THE CANADIAN WEST
IN FICTION

THE CANADIAN WEST
IN FICTION

EDWARD McCOURT

THE RYERSON PRESS
TORONTO WINNIPEG VANCOUVER

© EDWARD McCOURT, 1970 (Revised)

First published, March, 1949

Revised edition, April, 1970

ISBN 0-7700-6037-4

PRINTED AND BOUND IN CANADA

BY McCORQUODALE & BLADES PRINTERS LIMITED

The Prairie Provinces constitute the most homogeneous of the great natural geographic divisions within this country. In spite of the abutment of the Rocky Mountains on the western flank of Alberta, all three, in their settled areas, are primarily flat and agricultural; they are hot in summer and cold in winter and the wind blows hard and often across them. The sun sets over them in a blaze of colour beyond the comprehension of anyone unfamiliar with the prairies; and the great arch of northern lights is a common sight three-quarters of the year. The provinces are alike in heterogeneity of their people, the Anglo-Saxon constituting in each something less than half the population. All three are bordered by Americans on the south and a vast, virtually unexplored hinterland on the north. They are young, aggressive, and united in their hostility to Ontario.

There are, of course, differences between provinces. Saskatchewan is flatter than Alberta and less wooded than Manitoba, and the wind seems to blow harder there than anywhere else in Canada. Manitoba, possibly because it borders on Ontario, is less radical in politics than Alberta or Saskatchewan. But there is remarkable unity of spirit prevailing among prairie dwellers; and a way of life as distinctive as the region which fosters it.

It is the purpose of this book to examine some of the prose fiction written about the Canadian West by native Westerners and others, and to attempt an estimate of the extent to which it is an artistic re-creation of the prairie way of life. The discussion is limited to novelists who have written in English; and no attempt is made to examine all the work of any one writer but only such parts of it as are relevant to the subject.

It may be objected that the title, *The Canadian West in Fiction,* is inaccurate, since the most westerly province of all is not included in the discussion. But British Columbia is a world apart from the prairies: regional unity begins near Kenora and ends in the foothills. To the native of the prairies Alberta is the far West; British Columbia the near East.

It is customary to conclude a prefatory note such as this with a word of thanks to all who have in any way helped the author in the preparation of his manuscript. The word is always gracious, but not always wise; for those whose assistance is thus publicly acknowledged must assume at least some small share of responsibility for the author's work. I shall therefore thank only my wife, thus confining responsibility for this little book to those who should properly share it.

EDWARD MCCOURT

PREFACE TO THE REVISED EDITION

Most of the new material in this book deals with western authors who have made their mark within the past two decades. I have also taken the opportunity to re-write the concluding chapter in the light of certain economic developments I did not foresee twenty years ago, and to make a number of minor corrections and revisions in the text as a whole.

University of Saskatchewan　　　　　　　EDWARD MCCOURT

CONTENTS

The fur-traders and explorers of the Hudson's Bay and North-West Companies were the first white men in the West after La Verendrye. Some of these men, like David Thompson and Alexander Mackenzie, were well educated, and some were almost illiterate; but the records which they left behind them are nearly all alike in their attention to the factual and disregard of the ornamental. The early adventurers in the West were men of action who wrote as they lived, with a strict regard for essentials. Peter Pond, that "man of violent temper and unprincipled habits," did not know much about spelling, but his famous *Journal* is a model of clarity, the work of a man who keeps his eye fixed unwaveringly upon the object which he seeks to describe. Pond wastes not a single word, but records what he sees with a kind of photographic precision and simplicity. And what is true of Pond is true of most of his fellow traders and explorers. The journal that is compiled on the trail is not likely to be overladen with decorative detail; and even though it may later be rewritten, the most carefully polished final draft will preserve something of the succinctness of the original. Men like Pond and Thompson and Mackenzie are seldom trapped in the pitfalls which beset the journalist who has time to go the longest way round.

The missionary followed close on the heels of the explorer and fur-trader. He came with the Word of God on his lips and, one is tempted to feel, a goose-quill in his hand. The black-robed voyageur Father Lacombe, for fifty years a familiar figure on the Western plains; James Evans, inventor of syllabic writing for the Crees, who in another environment might have been a great philologist; Robert Terrill Rundle, who brought the Word to the Blackfeet of what is now Southern Alberta and whose earthly memorial is the nine-thousand-foot slab of granite which bears his name; George McDougall, who died in a blizzard in 1876; his son John, and a score of others of lesser renown wrote voluminously and often with a simplicity not unworthy of the book they cherished. Thus James Evans writes from his lonely mission station on the shores of Lake Winnipeg to his wife in Ontario: "You gave me a little paper class-meeting and why should not I enjoy the same privilege? I am sure it will be agreeable to your feelings. Well I can, through grace, say that I am sure God has deepened His blessed work in my own soul since I arrived here. I enjoy great peace of mind. My intercourse with God is not clouded but clear and satisfactory. I am endeavouring to seek after more of the mind which is in Christ. . . . The world is losing its charms. I would just as soon be buried in the depths of these wilds as in a populous city. I love society you know; but I trust that God knows I love the poor benighted heathen more and that Heaven is just as near the wilderness as Toronto." And Thomas Hulburt, carrying on Evans' work for the faith, tells of the death of his baby son in words which would not have disgraced Bunyan: "My little son, whom I never saw, made but a transient stay in this world on his way to a better. He died on the 18th of October, aged two months and seven days."

The fur-traders and missionaries had much to record. There were the innumerable details of daily existence—the unending search for food, the winter-long battle against storm and cold, the contacts, sometimes pleasant, frequently disagreeable, with the native tribes — prosaic details no doubt to the veteran Westerner but new and exciting to people living in the settled East or the Old Country. There were stirring adventures, too, for the Canadian West, before the railroad came with settlements clinging like ugly nodules along the stem which nourished them, was a raw and violent land. Wars were common in the old days among the Indian tribes, and both Indian and white man were liable to swift, unnatural death. And in the sixties and seventies of the last century, when it was found that the whisky trade was even more profitable than the fur trade and hardly more precarious, violence and disorder raged along the border country north to old Fort Whoop-Up, near the site of the present city of Lethbridge, and on into the Bow River Valley. The whisky traders were the most degraded of the flotsam that drifted in on the tide of Western movement. Sometimes, under the influence of their own commodity, they went berserk and slaughtered without pity. In 1873 a large band of the Indians of the Assiniboine tribe — men, women and children—were massacred in the Cypress Hills by drunken traders and wolf-hunters bent on recovering some horses which they mistakenly believed the Indians had stolen from them. But even a whisky trader may show signs of grace; and legend has it that at the time of the massacre big Abe Farwell risked his life to save an Indian girl whom after his fashion he loved.

The Mounties came West in 1874. For weeks and months they moved across the plains, faces swollen with mosquito bites, tempers on edge, the bright scarlet of their tunics fading in the hot sun and pelting rain. They brought with them the majesty of the Law — a Law that was not created on the spot to meet the crude demands of local necessity but one that carried with it the strength and dignity of a tradition extending back through Blackstone and Coke and the Petition of Right to Magna Carta. They built Fort Macleod at the junction of the Oldman and Belly rivers and spread out north, east and west. Their forts were military outposts in semi-hostile country, and most of the occupants of the posts were militarily minded. Caesar's *Commentaries* notwithstanding, the arts have never flourished in a military camp. Like the fur-traders and the missionaries, the Mounties were men of action, capable of astonishing feats of endurance and of a single-minded devotion to duty which has won the admiration of the world. But they were not much interested in anything beyond the performance of duty and typically military relaxation afterwards. The records of the North-West Mounted Police are, as one would expect, coldly official; so are most of the memoirs compiled by its members. But the raw stuff of romantic fiction was in the records. Once uncovered — Ralph Connor was the first to realize its potentialities — it was to provide a wealth of material which exploitation by pulp-writers of a score of countries could not exhaust, nor the blatant vulgarity of Hollywood wholly corrupt.

II

The earliest imaginative literature dealing with the Canadian West is the work of fly-by-night travellers, journalists, and romantic novelists whose knowledge of the prairies was at best seldom more than second- or third-hand. That it should be so is inevitable. The creation of a native regional literature is dependent in part upon the existence of a relatively populous and stable society, and there was no such society in Western Canada before the coming of the c.p.r. in 1884.

Most of the early settlers who followed the railroad into the West, particularly those of Anglo-Saxon stock, were highly literate and do not greatly resemble their counterparts on the Western frontier of the United States. If we rely on the evidence of Mark Twain and other more sober if less lively historians, the first public institution to be established in a typical American frontier community was the saloon, followed almost immediately thereafter by a cemetery. But in the Canadian West the first community institution seems to have been either a church or a police barracks; the second, one is tempted to feel, a Literary Society. The Fort Macleod Literary and Historical Society was founded as early as 1884 when the town was little more than a cattle trail with a few ramshackle buildings on either side. John Maclean, Methodist missionary to the Piegan Indians and biographer of James Evans, Captain Cotton of the North-West Mounted Police, and Frederick Haultain, later Premier of the North-West Territories, were the executive of the Society. At the opening meeting Mr. Maclean spoke on "Indian Literature," a more appropriate topic than the majority of those which found favour with the Literary Societies of the period. The Regina Literary and Music Society, founded in 1885, instituted an annual Burns' Night celebration in 1887. The popularity of the Burns' Night festival in many Western communities is one of the more obvious indications of the tendency of the average Literary Society to derive its stimulus from traditional rather than native sources.

Other indications of the emphasis placed by the early settlers interested in literature on traditional rather than indigenous culture are to be found in the literary controversies which from time to time enlivened the correspondence columns of the prairie newspapers. Almost invariably these controversies were concerned with the merits of established Old Country writers. Thus a reviewer who, in the pages of the Regina *Leader,* had the temerity to argue the superiority of a "Charge of the Light Brigade" by one Michael Joseph Barry over the Laureate's more familiar version, provoked a storm which extended far beyond the limits of the capital city, and agitated the columns of the Moosomin *Spectator* for several issues. A Mr. Basil Tempest entered the lists as Tennyson's defender; his defence, as recorded in the *Spectator,* took the form of a vitriolic and at times highly entertaining attack on poor Michael Barry. The spirit of Mr. Tempest's criticism is well illustrated in his comments on the concluding lines of Barry's poem:

> *On, on, their bloody path is spread*
> *Each step, with dying and with dead!*
> *But each proud rider's manly head*
> *Turns fearless, tow'rds the foe.*

"The last two lines," says Mr. Tempest, "are the gems of the tawdry collection. It would be singular if the riders' proud manly heads were not turned towards the foe considering that they were charging directly at them. No one has yet accused the British cavalry of going forth to battle with their faces towards their horses' tails." In the concluding paragraph of his letter he turns his attention to Barry's eulogist. "I offer no apology to the *Leader* critic for occupying so much of this letter with a criticism of Barry, for he himself has set the example, and, as he says that 'no man can criticize a poet who has not in himself the potentiality of a poet' I am constrained to believe that the limits of his potentiality coincide rather with the muse of the late lamented Michael Barry than with the infinitely higher strain of Tennyson."

It is to be regretted that Mr. Tempest—who is representative of a large, well-educated group of early settlers — wasted his genuine literary talents in such pointless controversy. Perhaps, had he taken the trouble to exercise his acid wit in a commentary on the local scene he would have earned for himself a respectable place in the ranks of Canadian satirists.

By the turn of the century the Literary Society was firmly rooted in many Western Canadian communities. But for obvious reasons it neither called into being nor gave impetus to any significant literary movement. Its function was primarily social. The members debated the comparative merits of town life and country life, the sword and the plough, the pulpit and the newspaper, topics which even in 1900 were hoary chestnuts; they listened to papers on Tennyson and Browning — usually read by the local minister — and entertained one another with musical selections. No doubt the refreshments constituted the most enjoyable part of the ordinary Literary Society programme. Insofar as the Society interested itself in creative writing its influence was probably detrimental, since it tended to encourage slavish imitation of existing models rather than the creation of a vigorous and authentic regional literature.

But although the literature of the early Canadian West is of little merit, it is surprisingly abundant. There were Literary Societies in every town and a Sarah Binks on every stook. Most of the verses which these prairie bards composed were highly imitative, first of Tennyson or Browning, later of Kipling, but some of them are still capable of inspiring pleasure, although hardly of the kind which their authors seem to have intended. Is it possible to read, for example, the following tribute to the c.p.r. engineer, published in a volume of collected "Works" at the turn of the century, and remain unmoved?

> *With dusty face and strong and steady hand*
> *He swiftly steers his snorting steaming steed*
> *Along the bright steel band*

Which joins our sunny land
To the shining sea.
And clothed in blue overalls is he.
He's a wife and child in Winnipeg city,
And he thinks,
With eyes full of coal-dust gritty
Of his baby's head
In her soft white bed.
And far to the eastward his dear ones be.
And in coarse cotton clad is he;
We are human freight
In this sleeper behind.
Still, his nerves are iron, so never mind.
But only pray that the fates be kind,
As far to the West through the night we flee—
To the man in the greasy suit, siree!
No tailor-made coat,
What does that matter?
As at our windows the hailstones patter,
Hark how the wheels of his mogul clatter,
On the downward grade.
A grimy trade?
Yes, perhaps that's so,
But then, you know,
Wore he white linen like you, you see,
Our wide west land, what would it be?

Other poets of the early West include Bertram Tennyson, nephew of the Laureate, whose collected "Works," published in Moosomin in 1896, are interesting as evidence that literary genius is not necessarily transmitted to nephews; and Isaac White, who wrote copiously "in the backwoods of Manitoba" and published his meditations in a volume which is still a peculiar treasure. *Manitoba Muses* contains no fewer than three epics on Old Testament themes; but in spite of this seeming preoccupation with Homer and the prophets, Mr. White is first and foremost a crusader bent on exposing the evils of inoculation:

A ruthless, callous-hearted band
Called Boards of Health—how false the name!
Just spread disease throughout the land,
Doctors to help to win to fame.
O Freedom, wilt thou come again
And children save from Health-Board men!
They force their virus on the poor,
The rich can them escape, and do;
Compulsion is a weapon sure,
That cuts the health and freedom too.
For how can people be called free,
When ruled by cruel tyranny? . . .

Vaccine and anti-toxin are
The worst disease you will find:
Not only do they make a scar—
They leave a bad disease behind.
Vile toxin is a blighting curse,
Compulsion makes pure vaccine worse.

The remaining poems in *Manitoba Muses* suggest an affinity between Mr. White and Julia Moore, whom Bill Nye hailed as the only poet he ever heard tell of who wrote with a Gatling gun. It is true that Mr. White does not approach the Sweet Singer of Michigan's score of fifteen killed and twenty-nine wounded in one slim volume, but his elegiac tributes to deceased members of the Royal Family and citizens of Neepawa, Manitoba, add up to a respectable total. The "Impromptu" occasioned by the death of Edward VII is a good example of Mr. White's more exciting mortuary verse:

Our King is dead!
Britain's beloved King is dead!
On the 6th of May his spirit fled.
Mourn, Empire, mourn: Our King is dead!

King Edward, idol of the world,
Peacemaker, benefactor, friend;
A model King, an honoured King,
But death his peaceful reign doth end.

The Empire mourns: what can it do,
But weep for loss of King so true?
A noble soul! Mourn, Empire sore,
King Edward's dead: His reign is o'er!

III

Although their muse was constantly and shrilly vocal, the poets of the early West were easily surpassed in bulk of output by the *raconteurs,* many of whom seem to have begun recording their impressions of the Great Lone Land while still *en route* to it. The records of such highly literate men as Butler, Palliser and Cheadle, who journeyed across the plains when the West was still Indian country, rank high in the literature of travel, but the settlers who followed them were more garrulous and less gifted. What they wrote—and in the closing decades of the nineteenth century they wrote a good deal — is now of little interest to anyone other than the professional scholar. There are, however, one or two notable exceptions, memoirs long since out of print and forgotten, but worthy of revival. One such book, misleadingly called *Trooper and Redskin,* by Lance-Corporal William Donkin of the North-West Mounted Police, might well be required reading of all those brought up in the romantic tradition of the Riders of the Plains.

Donkin came to Canada from India, where he had served for a time with a famous British cavalry regiment on the Northwest frontier. A few months' experience as hired man was enough to sicken him of farm life and, like many another restless spirit of similar background, he joined the Mounties. According to Donkin the North-West Mounted Police were, in 1884, "a splendid body of men with a fine contempt for civilians." "There were none of the questionable characters then," he explains, "who crept in when recruiting parties went through the slums of Ontario."

Donkin moved about a good deal — from Regina to Prince Albert, where he was stationed during the Riel Rebellion, and later to Manitoba. In *Trooper and Redskin* he describes his experiences without romanticizing them. He liked neither the country nor the people, and he does not hesitate to say so in terms which no doubt gave grave offence to many of his readers. He is our first Canadian realist. Few writers since Donkin have conveyed more effectively the sense of desolation and heart-breaking loneliness which the prairie scene communicates to the newcomer from the populous regions of America or the Old World:

The Indian teepee, the scattered tents of the mounted police; or, perhaps, the log house or sod shanty of some adventurous pioneer, are the only vestiges of human life out in these mighty solitudes. There is the hush of an eternal silence hanging over the far-stretching plains. In early summer, for a brief space, the prairie is green, with shooting threads of gold, scarlet and blue, while the odour of wolf-willow and wild rose floats through the clear air. But, by and by, the sun gains power and scorches and withers, with a furnace heat; and through the shimmering haze the grass lies grey and dead. And, under the merciless glare, a great silence broods over all. No tree or bush relieves the aching eye; there is nothing but the dim fading ring of the horizon all around. . . . In winter, it is more awful still, covered with one unbroken mantle of pure white; and stream and sleugh, pond and lake are locked in the stern grasp of ice. The starved coyote prowls through the wilderness and the howling, deathly blizzard revels in demon riot. No buffalo roam these pastures now, a few deer and prairie chicken are all the game. There is a terrible monotony and sameness in the aspect of the great American desert. . . . You may blindfold a man, and take him to another spot a hundred miles away; when, upon removing the bandage, he would simply think he had travelled around in a circle.

The general effect of this passage is so good that we can readily forgive Donkin his starved coyote and blizzard revelling in demon riot. At other times his comments on the Western scene are distinguished by a quality of dry, sardonic humour. His description of early Saskatoon is an effective bit of satiric anti-climax:

During the bustle of landing at Quebec, beset on every side by touts of every description, I found a pamphlet thrust into my hand by a clerical looking fellow in seedy dress. This paper-backed volume professed to show the glorious future which awaited anyone who took up land near the South Saskatchewan under the aegis of the Temperance Colonization Company.

There was even an illustration of Saskatoon, above the title of a North-West City. Tall chimneys were emitting volumes of smoke, there were wharves stocked with merchandise; and huge steamers such as adorn the levees at New Orleans were taking in cargo. Subsequently I found Saskatoon to consist of six houses at intervals, and a store.

Donkin's division of the Western Canadian year into five parts — the mosquito season, the black-fly season, the horse-fly season, the house-fly season and winter — has still some claims to validity. And certainly, were Donkin permitted to revisit the West, after a lapse of some eighty years, he would find no cause to revise his final stinging indictment of our culture: "In Canada there are no barmaids: society is not sufficiently educated for them."

It is not, perhaps, surprising that after three years' service Lance-Corporal Donkin of the North-West Mounted Police bought his discharge from the Force and returned to the Old Country to write his reminiscences. It is a pity that he did not try his hand at fiction. One suspects that had he done so he would have been our first realistic novelist.

IV

The most serious charge that may be laid against the host of Western Canadian memoir writers is that they failed to assess properly the value of the material at their disposal. Many of them foolishly tried to create the impression that the West of the 70's and 80's was a lawless land infested by Indians and bandits who menaced the life of the settler every time he went to the pasture for the cows. In part this tendency reflects the influence of American frontier literature which was legitimately exploiting the blood-curdling and sensational, in part the inability of our writers to comprehend the dramatic impact on character and ordinary human relationships of an environment whose most obvious characteristic was — and perhaps still is—monotony. In the same way our early Western novelists tended to play up exciting incidents at the expense of atmosphere and characterization: it was easier to do so, and more likely to win a large popular audience in the East and the Old Country.

In the late nineteenth century romantic tales about the Canadian West, many of them written for juveniles, enjoyed considerable popularity. Before 1885 most of these tales were the work of writers who were merely visitors to the Western frontier, or who — more frequently — relied wholly on their imaginations for the creation of a setting appropriate to tales of hair-raising adventure. Of the few local writers, men to whom the prairies were a familiar environment, the most widely known in his own time was Alexander Begg, remembered today not as a novelist but as the author of an acceptable history of the North-West. Begg's one novel, *Dot It Down* (so called after a conspicuous habit of one of the chief characters) is based on his experiences in the Red River settlement of Manitoba. The work has no artistic virtues; it is really an extended pamphlet which sets forth in fictional form the realities of pioneer life in the Red River Valley. Begg gives much sound advice in a palatable form; but at times his optimism gets the better of his judgment, as when he assures prospective settlers of wheat crops yielding up to seventy bushels to the acre. Historically, *Dot It Down* is of some interest since it anticipates the flood of pamphlet literature — most of which may be most accurately classed as fiction — later released by the railroad and land companies.

To the romantically minded would-be novelists of the West, the second Riel Rebellion of 1885 came as a godsend. Here at last in Canada was the kind of action that readers had become accustomed to associating only with the American frontier. Here was the blood and thunder they wanted to read about and were willing to pay for — whooping Indians on the warpath — settlers, white-faced, resolute, crouching behind barred doors — and across the dusty plains the Mounties and the militia riding unheard of distances to effect a stirring last minute rescue and restore the supremacy of the white man throughout the land. What matter if in actual fact the Riel Rebellion resolved itself into a series of petty skirmishes in which the militia gained some experience and no distinction; what matter if incompetence or jealousy at Military Headquarters rendered the Mounted Police virtually powerless for the duration of the campaign; what matter if, in the end, the real hero should be the shabby little Messiah, Louis Riel, whom judicial and governmental intransigence elevated to the role of martyr? What *did* matter was that the red-skins were at last on the war-path.

The first writer to exploit the situation which Riel's uprising had created was Edmund Collins, a Toronto man whose previously published fiction included a few short stories and a novelette, *Nancy, the Lightkeeper's Daughter.* Collins wrote *The Story of Louis Riel* while the rebellion of 1885 was still in progress. According to his own testimony, which no reader will feel inclined to dispute, the task occupied him seventeen days.

The Story of Louis Riel, although of no merit whatever, is of some interest since it gave rise to the curious legend that Riel had ordered the execution of young Thomas Scott in 1870 because Scott was his rival in love. So widely was this explanation of the seemingly unmotivated murder of Scott accepted in Eastern Canada that in the epilogue to his second thriller dealing with the rebellion, *Annette, the Metis Spy,* Collins was himself moved to disclaim any factual basis for the legend which he had unexpectedly created.

Annette, the Metis Spy, which Collins dedicated to Archibald Lampman, deals, as the title suggests, with the exploits of a Duck Lake Mata Hari. It is sufficient to say of *Annette* that it is in every way a worthy successor to *The Story of Louis Riel.* Collins even goes so far as to incorporate part of the earlier work into *Annette,* citing as justification the alleged practice of Thackeray. In his epilogue, which is surely one of the gems of early Canadian literature, he acknowledges that he has dealt rather cavalierly with Western Canadian topography:

I have arranged the geography of the Territories to suit my own conveniences. I speak of places that no one will be able to find on maps of the present or future. Where I want a valley or a swamp, I put the same: and I have taken the same liberty with respect to hills and waterfalls. The birds, and in some instances the plants and flowers of the prairie, I have also made to order.

But a disregard of the facts of history and a total ignorance of locale are not necessarily characteristics of all fiction written about the Riel Rebellion during the late nineteenth century. There were writers living in the West sufficiently familiar with the local scene to find the creation of their own flora and fauna unnecessary, and well enough versed in local history to know that Custer's last stand was not made in Manitoba, as the two Old Country ladies who wrote *The Red House by the Rockies* (published by the Society for the Propagation of Christian Knowledge) seem to have believed. But the blight of genteel literacy is upon all their works; and over the prairie landscape move Victorian dummies lifted straight out of the polite fiction of the Old Country, if anything a little more bloodless and refined than their originals.

V

Edmund Collins is representative of the novelists who wrote about the early West partly from experience but mostly from imagination. Their novels are forgotten now, and it is well that they should be. They provided pleasant entertainment in their time, no doubt, but their resurrection serves only to confirm the wisdom of leaving the dry bones of the dead to rest in peace. For none of these early writers had the ability or even the inclination to tell the story of the West as it took shape before their eyes, to make use of genuine local characters, local customs, and the profound psychological experiences of newcomers to a frontier community. Neither did they have the talent to tell a good straightforward adventure story for its own sake, in the manner of Marryat or Ballantyne. There is more meat, more exciting incident, more narrative skill in the records of a single missionary like Evans or John McDougall than in the entire body of fiction produced in and about the West before the turn of the century.

For the man with imagination the material was there, in the records of the fur-trader and missionary and policeman, in the struggle of the settler to establish himself in a new community, in the lives of ordinary men and women growing old in a world that was new. But it was not until the close of the century that any intelligent use was made of the rich material at hand. In the 1890's a young man came to the West, a Presbyterian missionary whose Celtic imagination caught fire in an environment which stirred him to fierce love, although never to complete understanding. And from the material which he found around him and transformed in the heat of his imagination, he fashioned a series of tales, which, to paraphrase his own words, were destined to make his name known wherever the English language was spoken.

In the winter of 1897 Charles William Gordon, a Presbyterian minister living in Winnipeg, sent a few sketches describing life in a British Columbia mining camp to his friend the Rev. James MacDonald, editor of the Presbyterian church paper, *The Westminster Magazine*. The readers of the *Westminster* liked the pieces so well that MacDonald was moved to a daring suggestion. "We'll make a book of the sketches," he said, "and publish a first edition of a thousand copies." One thousand copies of a book by an unknown Canadian to be printed in Canada was a hitherto unheard-of number. Mac-Donald's friends were quick to predict the failure of his undertaking. But *Black Rock,* by Ralph Connor (Gordon's *nom de plume* created through a telegrapher's misreading of Can. Nor., an abbreviation of Canadian North-West), sold five thousand copies in a few weeks and Canadian publishing history was made. Author and publisher were quick to follow up their unexpected success. The young minister's second volume of sketches, published in 1899, dealt with the foothills country of Alberta, where Gordon had for four years been in charge of a mission field in "the largest Presbytery in the world." The title of the collection was an inspired one, and the sales of *The Sky Pilot* ran into the thousands almost overnight. By the turn of the century Ralph Connor was Canada's most popular novelist. The "Glengarry" books, published in 1901 and 1902 and dealing with his own boyhood in Eastern Ontario, confirmed his position as the most successful writer

24

in Canadian literary history. *The Doctor,* published in 1906, sold 150,000 copies within three weeks of publication, without benefit of book clubs or extensive advertising campaigns. The total hard-cover sales of Ralph Connor's books have never been accurately estimated, but the figure is now well over five millions.

But *The Doctor,* in spite of its huge sales, was not received with the unrestrained enthusiasm which had welcomed its predecessors. The reviewers were not altogether kind. Specifically, they objected to what they felt to be the over-emphasis of purpose in the novel. "One might almost be justified in saying that *The Doctor* is Ralph Connor's best work," wrote the book editor of *The Canadian Magazine.* "If one were content to stop at the night when Barney entered Dick's bachelor apartment and found his trusted brother and Iola, his sweetheart, in passionate embrace — if one were content to stop there and read no further, the verdict would likely be that the author had exceeded himself. But it is, perhaps, the best word for the story that the reader is not content to stop there. Unfortunately, however, the latter half does not seem to ring true, and the denouement is anything but satisfactory. Maybe it suffers the fate of many so-called purposeful novels, and it is interesting to wonder whether the author has sacrificed the acclaim of posterity in order to serve what to him appears to be the present and higher duty."

Such a review reflects rather than anticipates a growing impatience on the part of critics and reading public with sermons in the guise of fiction. And although Ralph Connor's books continued to sell in scores of thousands for at least a decade after the publication of *The Doctor* he never again achieved the astounding success of his earlier books — *Black Rock, The Sky Pilot, The Man From Glengarry, Glengarry Schooldays,* and *The Prospector.* The decline of his reputation, most pronounced in the decade following the First World War, has continued without interruption. Today it is customary to dismiss Ralph Connor as a writer of inconsequential little moral tales which once enjoyed unwarranted popularity because they were created in a time more naive, more optimistic, and a good deal less critical than our own.

But a Canadian writer who has lived for well over half a century, whose name was once well-known throughout the English-speaking world, and whose books have sold in millions, cannot be thus summarily dismissed. Even if his books were now completely forgotten — many of them are still in print and enjoying a paper-back revival — he would be a phenomenon worthy of critical consideration. For through his novels he performed a very real service on behalf of the Canadian frontier. Even now, when conditions are appropriate to a sharing of confidences, to a half-ashamed, half-boastful confession of youthful *naïveté* and extravagance, many a white-headed business tycoon, many a superannuated clergyman and more than one college president will probably acknowledge that a boyhood reading of Ralph Connor drew him to the West. Indirectly, the author of *Black Rock* and *The Sky Pilot* was the West's most effective booster, his books better advertising material than anything ever dreamed up by harassed railroad or government publicity men.

It is easy now to understand why Ralph Connor enjoyed such popularity at the turn of the century. In books like *Black Rock, The Sky Pilot, The Prospector* and *The Doctor* he wrote of a locale which was in itself of absorbing interest to the ordinary Easterner or Old Country man. For the Canadian West was the last great frontier of the New World, an Empire within an Empire already absorbing immigrants at the rate of nearly fifty thousand a year and calling for more. It was a land of promise, a land of romance — by 1900 the tradition of the North-West Mounted Police had been firmly established — a land where it was possible, if need be, to forget the past and begin again. Unlike the northern frontier of today, which has not excited comparable interest, the West of fifty years ago was readily accessible and invited settlement. It was almost instinctive for the man seeking an opportunity to create a home for himself and his family to turn his thoughts and eventually his face west. And in the pages of *The Sky Pilot* and *Black Rock* and *The Prospector* he found much to encourage his dream.

For Ralph Connor, writing with the authority of a veteran western missionary, painted the West as the land of beginning again. The mining camps of British Columbia and the ranches of the foothills he peopled with many types, which tend to fall into two general categories, heroes and villains. The heroes behave in traditional fashion; so, up to a point, do the rogues and outcasts. But the evil-doers are seldom in the end destroyed; rather through the power of God they are transformed into repentant and respectable citizens. Such transformation is not always a deliberate sentimentalizing of character. For it was Ralph Connor's earnest conviction that in every man there is some element of good, some claim to God-hood which the right environment may bring into the light. So it is that he sees the West as a land where there is hope for even the weakest of the misfits of an older society. Nor is it altogether true to say that the kind of hope which Ralph Connor creates is a spurious one, born of false optimism and wishful thinking. It stems from passionate conviction which has its origin in temperament and its confirmation in experience. As missionary and clergyman he had seen, not once but many times, the startling regenerative effort of religious conversion. Men, he knew, could be changed. And the West, free from the restraints and conventions of an older society—simpler, more wholesome — provided the ideal environment for the change. By temperament sanguine, Ralph Connor found it easy to imagine the kind of transformation he had seen taking place in individuals being extended, under appropriate conditions, to entire groups. Hence the mass reforms and conversions which are a characteristic feature of several of his novels. No doubt the readers of an earlier day, to whom the West was a young and enchanted land, were readily persuaded that in the loneliness of the great open spaces a man found it easy to come to grips with his God.

The sincere faith with which Ralph Connor illustrates his doctrine of regeneration is reflected in his characters. They are extreme simplifications of good and evil, but there is nothing to show that the author is himself aware of the simplification. To the contrary he believes in his characters implicitly because in his own life he tended to see people in strong blacks and whites and outlines larger than human. His autobiography, *Postscript to Adventure,* overflows with superlatives. His father (the Rev. Alexander Murray of the Glengarry stories) "was indeed a great preacher. Not one of all the great preachers I have known could thrill my soul as could my father when I was a little lad." His brother Gilbert was a man "of magnificent physique and invincible pluck . . . strong, cool, quick, with a courage that nothing could daunt." Among his friends and fellow ministers not one was commonplace. Dr. Henry Drummond "had an amazing power to draw the best out of you. What a hero! He died like one. What a saint! He lived like one." And in the personality of the Rev. Dr. James Robertson, for twenty years superintendent of missions for the Presbyterian Church in the West "were to be found the qualities of a statesman — vision, organizing ability, power to inspire heroic deeds, selfless devotion to his country, a courage that never faltered and a persistence that never swerved from the line of duty."

It was inevitable that the combination of *naïveté* and hero-worship so apparent in these sketches of the people of Ralph Connor's real world should contribute to the creation of fictitious characters in whom there should be no shadings, no delicate nuances. But it must not be forgotten that they were given to the public at a time when the traditional conception of the frontiersman as a simple-hearted rugged individualist was still strong; and the average reader no doubt found, in Ralph Connor's missionaries and doctors and prospectors and outlaws-with-hearts-in-the-right-place, confirmation of his vague romantic notions. It is true that one querulous critic protested his inability to believe in a hero like Shock MacGregor of *The Prospector,* who was "an Apollo, a John Wesley and a Livingstone all in one." But such objections were rare. Ralph Connor's enthusiasm for his own characters was contagious. He himself knew and believed in Barney Boyle and the Sky Pilot and Corporal Cameron and Shock MacGregor; and his readers found it easy to share his conviction.

The women of Ralph Connor's novels are even more limited in range than the men. The men at least fall into two broad divisions—good and bad. But Ralph Connor created no "bad" women. One suspects that he found it hard to acknowledge the fact of their existence. And yet his stereotyped heroines, like so many of his heroes, carry a kind of conviction because their creator never doubts their reality. To him Mrs. Mavor of *Black Rock,* Lady Charlotte Ashley of *The Sky Pilot,* and Mrs. Murray of the Glengarry books are living persons because they are idealizations of his own mother. Ralph Connor never wrote his mother's formal biography; instead, he introduced her in fictitious guise into nearly every novel he wrote. Of the passionate sincerity of his devotion to her memory there can be no question. And the devotion was not misdirected. There is evidence to suggest that Mary Robertson was as remarkable a woman as Barrie's Margaret Ogilvy. Certainly she made it impossible for her son to think evil of any woman. And because so many of his characters are idealized projections of Mary Robertson he is sometimes able, through his own passionate belief in their reality, to persuade the reader that such women actually exist in the flesh.

When Ralph Connor tried to create a feminine character who was a departure from the type which early became conventional with him the results were usually unfortunate. Mandy Haley, the heroine of *Corporal Cameron,* is at first appearance a far cry from the traditional heroine of the author's earlier novels. She is a slatternly Ontario farm girl, ignorant, stupid, vaguely heartsick for the better things of life. The reader's — and Cameron's — first glimpse of her is unpleasant but convincing:

Turning, he saw a girl of about seventeen, with little grace and less beauty, but strongly and stoutly built, and with a good-natured if somewhat stupid and heavy face. Her hair was dun in colour, coarse in texture, and done up loosely and carelessly in two heavy braids, arranged about her head in such a manner as to permit stray wisps of hair to escape about her face and neck. She was dressed in a loose pink wrapper, all too plainly of home manufacture, gathered in at the waist, and successfully obliterating any lines that might indicate the existence of any grace of form, and sadly spotted and stained with grease and dirt. Her stout red arms ended in thick and redder hands, decked with an array of black-rimmed nails.

Her character is in keeping with her appearance. She is good-natured, slow-witted, with no apparent interests beyond the narrow confines of her physical existence. But because,

portrayed realistically, Mandy no doubt offended his conception of true womanhood, the author is unable to resist sentimentalizing his creation. Through the inspiring influence of
love Mandy is transformed in body, soul and intellect. When,
nearly two years after he has left the farm, Cameron again
sees her —

Before his eyes there floated an illusive vision of masses of
fluffy golden hair above a face of radiant purity, of deft fingers
moving in swift and sure precision . . . of two round capable
arms whose lines suggested strength and beauty, of a firm-knit,
pliant body that moved with an easy sinuous grace, of eyes—but
at the eyes he paused, forgetting all else, till, recalling himself,
he began again, striving to catch and hold that radiant, bewild-
ering elusive vision. That was a sufficiently maddening process,
but to relate that vision of radiant efficiency, strength and grace
to the one he carried of the farmer's daughter with her dun-
coloured straggling hair, her muddy complexion, her stupid
face, her clumsy, grimy hands and heavy feet, her sloppy figure,
was quite impossible. After long and strenuous attempts he
gave up the struggle.

So, unfortunately, must the reader. This is the kind of
fantastic implausibility which outrages the intelligence of even
the most uncritical romanticist. But, at least, acquaintance
with Mandy is sure proof of Ralph Connor's wisdom in
adhering to the type which he drew with love and conviction.
The re-emergence in novel after novel of the woman cast in
the mould of Mary Robertson suggests Ralph Connor's creative limitations; but it also suggests a recognition of those
limitations which—Browning to the contrary—is the beginning
of wisdom.

Perhaps the most obvious explanation of Ralph Connor's
popularity with readers not primarily interested in the Western frontier is to be found in his strong dramatic sense. That
sense operated within the strict limits of the physical. A
Highlandman by inheritance, Ralph Connor loved conflict.
As a small boy he listened with rapt attention to stories of the
wild Glengarry men of old and found in them inspiration
and material for many of the dramatic incidents of his novels.
"The tales of the fierce old days survived down into my times,"

he says, "stirring my youthful heart with profound regret that
deeds so heroically splendid should all be bad. For in spite
of the Great Revival we were of the same race, with the
ancient lust of battle in our blood." It is not surprising, in the
light of this confession, to find that Ralph Connor tends to
see life in terms of conflict on a simple level of physical strife.
For the Hamlet-like struggles of the human spirit within itself
he cares little. Good and evil are represented in his books by
hero and villain: the hero beats the villain to a pulp and the
villain as often as not benefits by his beating and reforms.
Even the simplest and most prosaic physical operation — the
raising of a barn, the binding of a grain-field — he turns into
a primitive battle in which Right and Justice invariably
triumph.

Nor can it be denied that Ralph Connor describes this kind
of simple, elemental conflict — hero against villain or against
the forces of nature — with a fine dramatic intensity. Even a
turnip-hoeing competition becomes an heroic struggle demanding epic phraseology for its description; and he must indeed
be a hardened reader who follows unmoved the progress of
twelve-year-old Tim Healey, Cameron's protégé, as he forges
ahead of Perkins (an unpleasant person who deserves a taking-
down) to win the unofficial county turnip-hoeing champion-
ship.

And surely nowhere else in literature, except possibly in
Tom Brown's Schooldays, are there such football games as in
the pages of Ralph Connor. The match between Varsity and
McGill, described in the second chapter of *The Prospector,* is
a classic of its kind; although some readers may prefer the
brief paragraph in *Postscript To Adventure* which describes
the actual game on which the fictitious account is based:

The story of the football match in Ralph Connor's *Prospector*
gives a true picture of a terrific struggle, not with McGill, however, but with a band of savage Irishmen from Ottawa College
who played to win regardless of rules and regulations and reck-
less of life and limb, their own or the enemy's. In spite of their
unscrupulous tactics, they were a great football team. It was a
joy to meet them on the field, a glorious triumph to defeat them,
and no shame to be beaten by them.

The effectiveness of a description of athletic competition is in part dependent on the sincerity of the author. Certainly Ralph Connor never saw a football game as a rather ridiculous exercise in which two teams of young men spend a futile afternoon pushing each other about a field while endeavouring to carry a ball across a white line. A football game was to him a stern test not only of a man's physical, but also of his moral, attributes. Thus when Cameron, the Scottish full-back, through a moment's fatal hesitation loses the game for his country to Wales, he is guilty not merely of bad football but of a moral lapse as serious in its way as Lord Jim's desertion of his ship, and equally demanding of a great act of atonement. And since it is human to enjoy physical combat so long as one is not personally involved, it is easy to understand Ralph Connor's appeal to the kind of audience which today gets its vicarious thrills from telecast showings of mayhem on the ice in the Maple Leaf Gardens.

Finally, in the sum of things which help to account for Ralph Connor's early reputation, the patriotic element in his work cannot be ignored. He was not a jingo patriot in the conventional sense, but his novels do express a serene confidence in the ability of the Briton—and particularly the North Briton — to bear the White Man's Burden in the new land of the West and to extend his control over the lesser breeds without the law in a manner beneficial to both ruler and ruled. He acknowledges that in the Canadian West the Indian has not always been fairly dealt with, but he clearly feels that occasional injustice and exploitation are more than compensated for by the protection which the Empire extends to even the humblest of its subjects. Nor does he seem aware of the ironic paradox implicit in much of his work, that the greatest menace from which the Indian must be protected is the white man. When the outlaw Raven, a cultured Old Country black sheep, risks his freedom and perhaps his life in order to help frustrate a rising of the Blackfeet in support of Riel, he speaks for his creator when he says that he is "not quite prepared to hand over this country to a lot of bally half-breeds and savages." In thus helping to maintain the supremacy of the white man he presumably makes atonement for a number of

venial sins, including whisky-running and murder. Ralph
Connor was a humanitarian, a man who despised cruelty and
oppression in every form. In an age when, as Lytton Strachey
has it, imperialism was a faith as well as a business, his
confidence in the generally beneficent nature of the white
man's rule was no doubt reassuring to his readers in Eastern
Canada and the Old Country.

II

It was inevitable that Ralph Connor should be the victim of a
reaction as disproportionate as the enthusiasm which had
greeted his books at the beginning of the century. The reaction
was intensified by the spiritual depression which followed the
First World War. In the decade of the twenties, the decade of
Hemingway and T. S. Eliot and the Lost Generation, there
was no place for the optimism and serene faith of a naive
prairie missionary. Ralph Connor's autobiography, *Postscript
to Adventure,* published in 1938, attracted little attention. Its
readers were the men of a former generation, and they read it
in the hope of re-kindling emotions which had been dead for
many years.

It is natural that the reader who knew and loved Ralph
Connor long ago, and who now seeks to appraise him with
some objectivity, must hesitate to take down from their shelves
the worn volumes in their characteristic black-lettered red
binding to read again tales which half a century ago were, to
the adolescent at least, just as thrilling as *Treasure Island* and
King Solomon's Mines and much more real. Such hesitation is
justified. For many of the great reading experiences of a man's
life, and especially those of boyhood, are so by happy accident
— because a particular book and a particular mood or age are,
for the time of reading, in absolute harmony. But because
such harmony can be rarely, if ever, achieved more than once
it is always dangerous to re-read books which were a peculiar
treasure in childhood. So it is that the mature reader must feel
that *Corporal Cameron* and *The Sky Pilot* and *The Patrol of
the Sun Dance Trail* belong in the catalogue of books to be
remembered fondly and left undisturbed on their shelves.

Assuredly a re-reading of Ralph Connor calls to our attention a score of obvious and distressing faults. There is, above all, his agonizing sentimentality. Like Dickens he at times ceases to be a rational being who brings the steadying light of intelligence to bear on all that he writes. Instead he from time to time abandons himself to a shameless wallowing in emotion. Few of his deathbed scenes can be read without a sense of the most acute embarrassment. It is in such scenes that Ralph Connor — in spite of the evidence of his own tears — is open to a charge that cannot often be laid against him, that of insincerity. The danger inherent in this kind of writing, in which the author abandons himself to the control of his emotions, has been pointed out most explicitly by Joseph Conrad:

In order to move others deeply we must deliberately allow ourselves to be carried away beyond the bounds of our normal sensibility, innocently enough, perhaps, and of necessity, like an actor who raises his voice on the stage above the pitch of natural conversation — but still we have to do that. And surely this is no great sin. But the danger lies in the writer becoming the victim of his own exaggeration, losing the exact notion of sincerity, and in the end coming to despise truth itself as something too cold, too blunt for his purpose — as, in fact, not good enough for his insistent emotion. From laughter and tears the descent is easy to snivelling and giggles.

Ralph Connor's sentimentality is not, unfortunately, confined to individual scenes; it tends to permeate all his work. It expresses itself, for instance, in the ease with which he assumes the innate goodness of man and the ultimate working out of all things on earth for the best. To a generation to whom Buchenwald and Hiroshima and the gas-chambers of Oswiecim and Birkenau are monstrous facts, the devil in man is at least as obvious as the god. Yet it is possible that some readers may find in Ralph Connor the vision of the prophet. Says Old Man Nelson, a typical *Black Rock* down-and-out, to Mr. Craig, the minister, who is calling on him to follow Christ, "If this is no good it's hell for me." And the minister replies, "If it's no good it's hell for all of us."

Paradoxically, Ralph Connor's limitations are sometimes

responsible for his best writing. He lacked inventive power, or at least patience to create fictitious incidents. Instead he relied for his material almost entirely upon incidents drawn from his own rich and crowded experience, and on characters whom he had known in life. *Glengarry Schooldays* is a dramatized account of his own boyhood. *The Sky Pilot* and *Black Rock* and *The Prospector* are founded on his experiences as missionary in the foothills. "I knew the country. I had ridden the ranges. I had pushed through the mountain passes. I had swum my broncos across its rivers. I had met the men — Hi Kendal and Bronco Bill and the rest were friends of mine." His best minor characters are undoubtedly these friends of his. Hi Kendal and Bronco Bill, the cowpunchers who provide most of the comedy relief in *The Sky Pilot,* are no doubt over-simplified, but Ralph Connor succeeds in making the reader feel their *naïveté,* their childlike wonder in the presence of anything outside the scope of their immediate environment. Bill's interpretation of Biblical narrative in terms of his own life is rendered with skill and insight. Thus Saint Paul, "the little chap who got mixed up in a riot and stood off a whole gang of thieves and cut-throats," is, in Bill's eyes, a stout-hearted Westerner involved in a saloon brawl who conducts himself in a manner worthy of the traditions of the frontier. It is, too, an accurate reflection of Bill's character that when an agnostic challenges his unquestioning acceptance of the Biblical story, Bill retorts by giving his tormentor a sound thrashing. Unfortunately the reader is left with the impression that Ralph Connor, too, considers the clenched fist the best of all possible replies to the doubter.

So long as Ralph Connor is content to deal with the simplified types whom he knew well in life his characters have some reality. Occasionally, too, he achieves an effective imitation of a type made familiar to him through his reading of Dickens. Mr. Rae, the family solicitor in *Corporal Cameron,* is an eccentric, tagged, like Uriah Heep, by a physical peculiarity:

An amazing smile was Mr. Rae's; amazing both in the suddenness of its appearing and the suddenness of its vanishing. Upon a face of supernatural gravity, without warning, without beginning, the smile, broad, full and effulgent, was instantaneously present. Then equally without warning and without fading the smile ceased to be. Under its effulgence the observer unfamiliar with Mr. Rae's smile was moved to a responsive geniality of expression, but in the full tide of the emotion he found himself suddenly regarding a face of such preternatural gravity as rebuked the very possibility or suggestion of geniality. Before the smile Mr. Rae's face was like a house, with the shutters up and the family plunged in gloom. When the smile broke forth every shutter was flung wide to the pouring sunlight, and every window full of flowers and laughing children. Then instantly and without warning the house was blank, lifeless and shuttered once more, leaving you helplessly apologetic that you had ever been guilty of associating anything but death and gloom with its appearance.

But most of Ralph Connor's imitations of literary types are not so inoffensive as Mr. Rae. He wrote at his best when he drew his stories and characters from his own experience, at his worst when he was self-consciously the man of letters. *The Doctor* is an unhappy example of a novel written in accordance with what the author seems to have thought was the mode of the hour. The story begins in a manner familiar to the reader of the earlier Connor. The hero, Barney Boyle, is a rugged Ontario farm boy haunted by the dream of becoming a great surgeon. The heroine, Margaret Robertson, is in the traditional mould, the author even going so far this time as to give her his mother's maiden name. The early chapters contain typical accounts of a barn-raising and a grain-binding competition, both described with characteristic lavish use of superlatives. But a new note is struck with the introduction of the *femme fatale* in the form of the beautiful, talented school-ma'am, Iola Lane. Iola is sensuous, passionate, and spiritual. Barney falls in love with her; and expresses his love in a manner which seems to be typical at one time or another of nearly all Ralph Connor heroes, through his fists. He hears Iola's name being lightly bandied at a Medical Association dinner and rises to her defence. The ensuing slaughter is awful to behold. Having literally wiped the floor with the besmirchers of Iola's name, Barney rages up and down in a fury that intimidates — as well it might — an entire roomful of besotted medical men:

He walked up and down before the group which stood huddled in the corner in abject terror, more like a wild beast than
a man. "You're not fit to live! You're beasts of prey! No decent
girl is safe from you!" His voice rose loud and thin and harsh.
He was fast losing hold of himself. His ghastly face, bloody and
horribly disfigured, made an appalling setting for his blazing
eyes. Nearer and nearer the crowd he walked, gnashing and
grinding his teeth till the foam fell from his lips. The wild fury
of his Highland ancestors was turning him into a wild beast
with a wild beast's lust for blood. Further and further back
cowered the group without a word, so utterly panic-stricken
were they.

It would seem that absurdity could go no further. But the
scene in which Barney chastises the entire Medical Society is
almost tolerable by comparison with the one in which he
resists Iola's seductive wiles and refuses to take advantage of
her willingness to surrender herself to him.

In fairness to Ralph Connor it must be pointed out that he
seldom exceeded the limitations which his lack of creative
power imposed upon him. The secret of his success lay partly
in the fact that — in the early years at least — he did not
consider himself a novelist at all, and hence did not dissipate
his powers in attempted inventions for which he had neither
liking nor talent. It was only after he had become conscious
of his position as a man of letters and tried to live up to it
that he perpetrated the kind of absurdity in which *The Doctor*
abounds.

Just as his best characters are simplifications of people whom
he knew in real life, so his most exciting bits of descriptive
writing are drawn from personal experience. The description
of frontier funeral mores in *The Sky Pilot* is one of the best
things in our Western literature. It deserves to be quoted in
full:

In the old times a funeral was regarded in the Swan Creek
country as a kind of solemn festivity. In those days, for the most
part, men died in their boots and were planted with much
honour and libation. There was often neither coffin nor shroud,
and in the far West many a poor fellow lies as he fell, wrapped
in his own or his comrade's blanket.

It was the manager of the xl Company's ranch who introduced crepe. The occasion was the funeral of one of the ranch cowboys, killed by his bronco, but when the pall-bearers and mourners appeared with bands and streamers of crepe, this was voted by the majority as "too gay." That circumstance alone was sufficient to render the funeral famous, but it was remembered, too, as having shocked the proprieties in another and more serious manner. No one would be so narrow-minded as to object to the custom of the return procession falling into a series of horse-races of the wildest description, and ending up at Latour's in a general riot. But to race with the corpse was considered bad form. The "corpse-driver," as he was called, could hardly be blamed on this occasion. His acknowledged place was at the head of the procession, and it was a point of honour that that place should be retained. The fault lay clearly with the driver of the XL ranch sleigh, containing the mourners (an innovation, by the way), who felt aggrieved that Hi Kendal, driving the Ashley team with the pall-bearers (another innovation), should be given the place of honour next the corpse. The XL driver wanted to know, in the name of all that was black and blue, what the Ashley ranch had to do with the funeral? Whose was the corpse anyway? Didn't it belong to the XL ranch? Hi, on the other hand, contended that the corpse was in charge of the pall-bearers. "It was their duty to see it right to the grave, and if they were not on hand, how was it goin' to get there? They didn't expect it would git up and get there by itself, did they? He didn't want no blanked mourners foolin' round that corp till it was properly planted; after that they might git in their work." But the XL driver could not accept this view, and at the first opportunity slipped past Hi and his pall-bearers and took the place next the sleigh that carried the coffin. Hi might have borne the affront and loss of position with even mind, but the jeering remarks of the mourners as they slid past triumphantly could not be endured, and the next moment the three teams were abreast in a race for dear life. The corpse-driver, having the advantage of the beaten track, soon left the other two behind running neck and neck for second place, which was captured finally by Hi and maintained to the graveside, in spite of many attempts on the part of the XL's. The whole proceeding, however, was considered quite improper, and at Latour's, that night, after full and bibulous discussion, it was agreed that the corpse-driver fairly distributed the blame. "For his part," he said, "he knew he hadn't ought to make no corp git any such move on, but he wasn't goin' to see that there corp take second place at his own funeral. Not if he could help it. And as for the others, he thought that the pall-bearers had a blanked sight more to do with the plantin' than them giddy mourners."

We can only regret that there is so little of this kind of writing in Ralph Connor. By comparison, the conventional sentimental account of the burial of the Pilot is made all the more unpalatable to the present-day reader.

Ralph Connor's descriptions of landscape are commonplace and without flavour. It is impossible to claim for him the discerning eye or sensitive imagination. His descriptive passages are neither photographic, in the sense that they record precisely the physical details of a scene, nor suggestive in that they give sentience to the inanimate. He sketches his Western pictures in vague generalities that with a little transposing could be adapted to suit any foothills landscape, as in the following characteristic passage:

What a morning it was! How beautiful our world seemed! About us rolled the round-topped, velvet hills, brown or yellow or faintly green, spreading out behind us to the broad prairie, and before, clambering up to meet the purple bases of the great mountains that lay their mighty strength along the horizon and thrust up white, sunlit peaks into the blue sky. On the hillsides and down in the sheltering hollows we could see the bunches of cattle and horses feeding upon the rich grasses. High above, the sky, cloudless and blue, arched its kindly roof from prairie to mountain peaks and over all, above, below, upon prairie, hillsides and mountains, the sun poured his floods of radiant yellow light.
As we followed the trail that wound up and into the heart of these rounded hills and ever nearer to the purple mountains, the morning breeze swept down to meet us, bearing a thousand scents, and filling us with its own fresh life. One can know the quickening joyousness of these Foothill breezes only after he has drunk with wide-open mouth, deep and full of them.

There is a suggestion, certainly, of spaciousness and colour here, but nothing more. The landscape lacks individuality; and nowhere in this passage is there a phrase — as there must be in great descriptive writing—which suggests that the author was looking at the scene through his own eyes and recording what was visible to him alone.

III

If we agree with Virginia Woolf that the business of the novelist is to create character, then Ralph Connor is not a novelist; if we agree with Arnold Bennett that the business of the novelist is to tell the truth in the form of fiction, then Ralph Connor is not a novelist; if we agree that the novelist's only obligation is to tell a good story, then Ralph Connor is not a novelist, for his books lack unity and tend to resolve themselves into a series of episodes loosely strung together. In a way, his popularity in his own time seems to have been as much a matter of shrewdness as of talent: he was sufficiently alert to see the value of material which had hitherto been neglected, and the human interest appeal of types hitherto largely unrecorded — the Mountie, the missionary, the remittance-man, the oldtimer. He had a keen eye for the obvious in character, situation and landscape, and the ability to record it in generalities comprehensible and agreeable to the ordinary reader. Finally, the emphasis on the Christian way of life so characteristic of all that he wrote, gave many readers the satisfying feeling that in addition to enjoying themselves they were experiencing genuine spiritual uplift. Ralph Connor was himself fully aware of the effect of this strong religious sentiment which pervades his books. He says:

Another cause of the phenomenal editions of these Ralph Connor books, and a very influential cause, was the fact that though in fiction form they possess a definitely religious motif. Religion is here set forth in its true light as a synonym of all that is virile, straight, honourable and withal tender and gentle in true men and women. And it was this religious motif that startled that vast host of religious folk who up to this time had regarded novel-reading as a doubtful indulgence for Christian people. I have received hundreds of letters expressing gratitude for a novel that presented a quality of religious life that "red-blooded" men could read and enjoy.

But for none of these reasons is Ralph Connor likely to be read today or in the future. The Mountie has become a stock character of Canadian and American popular fiction. His habitat, the West, is no longer a land of romance because it is the last frontier, the last frontier having shifted a thousand miles north. Nor — although it is still true that the student on a mission-field who can play baseball or run a fast hundred yards is more likely to have a full church than one whose interests are less "red-blooded"—is Christianity of the muscular variety as popular nowadays as it was fifty years ago. And even a generation brought up on soap operas is likely to find Ralph Connor's sentimentality out of date, just as his Doctor, Barney Boyle, lacks the glamour interest of the Caseys and Kildares and Corwins who weekly display their professional and other talents on TV.

And yet, one hardly dares predict oblivion for *The Sky Pilot*. Paradoxically the secret of Ralph Connor's astonishing vitality may lie in the fact that he was a novelist second, a man with a message first. Like the preacher of all ages he tells a tale to point a moral. Nor is the practise always artistically indefensible as *The Pardoner's Tale* bears witness. What Ralph Connor's son, King Gordon, has finely said of his preaching, is in part true of his books. "The secret of his power lay in his awareness of the tremendous mission of the church in desperate times and in the imaginative qualities of heart and mind which may well be the very essence of the life of the spirit."

And even those who deny everything that Ralph Connor preached, who detest his crudities and flinch from his breaches of good taste, who deride the simplicity of his character and the genial optimism of his faith, must recognize that intense spiritual awareness, which, however distorted in the presentation, gives his novels a passionate sincerity rare in Canadian literature. Whatever Ralph Connor's faults — and they are legion — it must be said of him as he said of his own Sky Pilot, that he had a true man's heart and a great purpose in it.

In 1918 the English novelist and critic, W. L. George, wrote an interesting little essay, "Who Is the Man?," in which, after acknowledging the then undisputed leadership in the field of the English novel of Arnold Bennett, Joseph Conrad, John Galsworthy, Thomas Hardy and H. G. Wells, he raised the question of succession. "Now not one of these men is under forty; one is over seventy; one approaches sixty. They must be replaced. Not yet, of course, though some of the young begin, a little rashly, to cast stones at those mature glories. But still, some time, we must ask ourselves: Who are the young men who rear their heads above the common rank? Which ones among them are likely to inherit the purple?"

Mr. George suggests, as obvious choices, J. D. Beresford, Gilbert Cannan, E. M. Forster, D. H. Lawrence, Compton Mackenzie, Oliver Onions and Frank Swinnerton. These are novelists who, George says, have "affirmed themselves earlier than did their seniors and quite as definitely." But he adds a second list, composed of the names of "obscurer" favourites, young intellectual novelists or more specialized men, "such as Mr. Algernon Blackwood, Mr. Frederick Niven or Mr. James Stephen, or a recent discovery such as Mr. Alec Waugh, Mr. J. W. N. Sullivan, Mr. Stephen McKenna or Mr. James Joyce."

Neither list suggests that W. L. George was a particularly acute critic. About all that can be said of his predictions is that they record an average number of hits and misses. But it is interesting to find Frederick Niven, whom we have come to look upon as a Canadian novelist, included in the list; for mention of his name in a work of popular criticism without explanatory comment suggests something of the reputation which he enjoyed fifty years ago when he was writing voluminously and at the height of his power.

This reputation Niven won largely through a single novel, *Justice of the Peace,* published in 1914. Always a prolific writer in spite of a hampering lack of inventive skill, he had written much else besides; and one earlier novel, *A Wilderness of Monkeys,* had won high praise from discerning critics. But *Justice of the Peace* called forth astonishing encomiums, many critics finding in it qualities which gave it rank among the most important novels of the twentieth century. Hugh Walpole, always kindly disposed towards his contemporaries, pays his compliments, in passing, to Niven's earlier novels, but it is for *Justice of the Peace* that his highest praise is reserved:

I believe that there is no novel in the English language in which Glasgow is so marvellously rendered. The close streets, the smoky air, the sky thick with moving cloud, the tea-shops with their surging customers, the strange mixed whirl of Art and Presbyterianism, the little pictures of Scottish country life, all these things compose one beautiful whole. . . .

Here is a writer who matters. It is time somebody came along and wrote an essay about Mr. Niven's Scottish novels, and if I were a collector of modern editions I would hurry along immediately and secure Firsts of *Ellen Adair, Two Generations,* and *Justice of the Peace.*

Born in Valparaiso, Chile, in 1878, of Scottish parentage, Niven was educated in Glasgow. He attended the Glasgow School of Art; and after a year or two in the Glasgow Public Library visited the Canadian West. His experience in the West provided him with material for several thrillers, including the very successful *Lost Cabin Mine,* and *Hands Up!* Back in Great Britain, Niven did newspaper work in Fleet Street. While employed as a professional journalist he found time to write two novels which were labelled Stevensonian by the critics, and the first of his realistic studies of Scottish life and temperament, *A Wilderness of Monkeys. Ellen Adair* and *Justice of the Peace* followed shortly, along with a miscellaneous assortment of thrillers, romantic narratives, and journalistic bits and pieces. But he could not forget the Canadian West and in 1920 he left Fleet Street for good. In a little poem written at Willow Point, Kootenay Lake, in 1924, he explains why:

> From humming-birds to sleigh-bells
>   I love the way life goes
> In this lost land, from one view,
>   But Paradise for those
> Who love the world God gave men,
>   Its Summers and its Snows.

Settled in British Columbia in the maturity of his powers Niven continued to write in two characteristic though disparate veins his solid stories of Scottish life and character under such forthright titles as *Old Soldier* and *The Staff at Simson's,* and Wild West thrillers intended for an audience more interested in action than art. He collaborated, as a labour of love, with the artist W. J. Phillips in a fine book about the Rockies — Niven always had a profound and deeply poetic feeling for mountains — thought a good deal and planned ambitiously. Not, perhaps, as ambitiously as Milton who early meditated the writing of a book which the world would not willingly let die — Niven was a modest man who never overestimated his powers — but bravely none the less and with a merited confidence. The plan which took root in his mind was one which no native writer had attempted to execute — the telling of the story of the Canadian West, in the form of fiction, from the days of the earliest settlements to the twentieth century. There was much good sense in the plan since it would enable Niven to combine in the same work his diverse creative talents. His taste for Wild West adventure would find legitimate scope and at the same time be restrained within the limits of the historical framework. The form of the historical novel could thus be used as a device to combine extravagant romance with sober reality.

This ambitious project was almost completed by the year of Niven's death. It took the form of a trilogy of novels, *The*

Flying Years (1935); *Mine Inheritance* (1940); and *The Trans-planted* (1944). Niven wrote much of *The Transplanted* during his last illness, a circumstance which no doubt accounts for the marked inferiority of the book to the other volumes of the trilogy. The value of Niven's contribution to the literature of the Canadian West must therefore be judged on the evidence of *The Flying Years* and *Mine Inheritance*.

II

What is the measure of Niven's accomplishment? One feels that in spite of his admirable technical equipment, the writing of the trilogy imposed too great a strain on his talents. In *The Flying Years* his canvas is a vast one — the Canadian West and its people from the time of the fur-traders to the twentieth century. It is a canvas so crowded with detail, each detail lovingly and accurately painted, that the picture as a whole is distracting in its variety and lack of emphasis. In outline the story is a simple one. The young Scot Angus Munro comes to Canada with his parents following their eviction from their Highland home in Brendan. They settle in the Red River district and there Mrs. Munro soon dies, crying out in her last hours for the hills of home. Three months later Daniel Munro joins his wife. Angus, alone in the world now, goes farther West, joins forces with Sam Douglas, an entrepreneur with the soul and hustle of a Yankee pedlar; works for the Hudson's Bay Company; marries a beautiful Indian girl Minota who bears him a child and dies of a white man's sickness; and after a time returns to Scotland with Douglas in order to raise money for the founding of a Western transport company. When no money is forthcoming he becomes a clerk in the bookstore of the Ettrick Brothers, Lothian Street, Edinburgh. But not for long. A chance encounter on the streets of Edinburgh with three Indians who are part of a New World exhibition revives old memories. In what is perhaps the best scene in the book he tenders his resignation to the Ettrick Brothers, and so returns to the only life which he finds more than merely endurable. Back in the Canadian West, Angus Munro works as Indian agent on a reservation; marries Fiona

Fraser whom he had known in the old Red River days; watches the rise of his old friend Sam Douglas to fortune and a peerage; sees his own son grow to manhood and march away to die in the First World War; and in old age lives on alone with only the memories of the Flying Years, within which the West developed to maturity, to comfort him.

Even such a brief outline as the foregoing suggests the chief defect of *The Flying Years*. The work is episodic; it suffers from lack of judicious selection of incidents and impressions. The steady succession of scenes, some momentous, many trivial, related only insofar as they are a part of Western Canadian history and not in the sense of having something to do with the characters, becomes wearisome in the end. Far from illuminating the characters it tends to obscure them. Niven's failure in *The Flying Years* is thus chiefly a failure in selection. He does not choose from the mass of material at his disposal the episodes which are significant in that they reveal and develop character. The characters are actually dwarfed by the background and at times entirely lost sight of in the welter of scenes and incidents, which, however accurately they may be recorded, are none the less artistically superfluous and hence harmful. This is a pity, for some of the people—Angus Munro, Sam Douglas — are potentially interesting. But the reader never feels that these are people who make history; rather, they are people to whom history happens.

The merit of *The Flying Years* is thus more nearly academic than artistic. It is a document rather than a novel, which describes with admirable fidelity the development of the West and some of the types who assisted in that development. But artistically it is a comparative failure; it is not memorable for character or plot, nor is it redeemed by a view of life which gives meaning to the movements of its people.

But there are things in *The Flying Years* hard to forget; notable among them being the superb passage of descriptive prose which records Angus Munro's first impressions of the Rocky Mountains:

Before him the Rocky Mountains were suddenly revealed beyond belts of colour that were of woods, parklands, wedges of sky-reflecting water, twist of river, fragment of distant lake. Very much as it was with him when listening to music was it with him then, gazing on the scene before him. Music would pick and choose through the past years of his life, recover and toss him this, that and the other: the tone of a voice, the light on a pebble, a forgotten wail of wind in a chimney from a winter storm of years back, the glance of eyes (Jessie's no doubt), the gleam through water of a herring shoal — and leave it to him to make something of the medley.

He thought of his father's remark — *Scotland, a kingdom of the mind.* Scotland was not his. They would not have him there. Well, he had Scotland still, the bark of seals on the Black Rocks, the remembered smell of sun-scorched bracken, of peat-smoke beaten down in the glades. He thought of the vast Atlantic swaying like a compass disc betwixt the rise and fall of Scotland's seaweed fringe and the scent of pines, firs and cedars in the mists off Newfoundland. Of the curve of the Milky Way he thought, seen from their prairie camps at night, a whirl and whiplash of light, up to the zenith and gone, of the Aurora Borealis, seen after hot summer days of their journey (not only in winter as many believed), he thought as he reined in his horse and sat motionless staring from that butte beyond Gull Lake at the revelation of the Rocky Mountains.

Something happened to him beyond his power to express; something happened, wordless, like music. As though the blue of the sky had run, and thickened roughly at the base, there lay the ranges, low in contrast with the height of that space of blue but — he aware of how far off they were — majestic in their serene extent. They dropped away to south, they dropped away to north, as into a quiet eternity. Here and there slashes of white showed among their purple. Here and there rocky gables twinkled like mirrors, and at one place, far in, there was a dun seething, peaks turning into cloud and clouds solidifying into peaks. A lightning flash was drawn in quick gold on that portion where peaks and clouds fused, and then came a distant sound, the faintest rumble.

And there is magic in the phrase "out of sight of land" as Niven uses it to describe the isolation of the traveller lost in the sea of grass which was the prairie, with "no lone butte even raising far off a purple knob in the immensity."

III

A reading of *Mine Inheritance* intensifies the feeling, created by *The Flying Years,* that in Niven's work we are witnessing something attempted on the grand scale, not quite successfully. In *Mine Inheritance* the scale is smaller than in *The Flying Years*, but still large. The action begins in the year 1811 with the arrival of one of the first groups of colonists from Scotland into the Red River settlement, recently established by the visionary Lord Selkirk. Niven describes in some detail the subsequent trials of the colonists, more especially those resulting from the antagonism of the stormy and resentful North-West Company fur-traders and their half-breed allies. The story closes on a comparatively serene note; the worst trials of the colonists are over, and peace of a kind prevails throughout the settlement. The action covers nearly twenty years, from 1811 to 1827.

Besides being conceived on a smaller and hence more workable scale than *The Flying Years, Mine Inheritance* has a unity of theme derived from the struggle of the colonists to establish themselves in the face of the most intense opposition from man and nature, which the earlier book lacks. And yet, Niven's failure to clothe dead bones and make them live again is even more marked than in *The Flying Years*. The historical background, in terms of a faithful recording of events in the order in which they occurred, is again impeccable. For the writing of the novel Niven did an immense amount of preparatory reading and research; and the bibliography appended to the novel lists nearly one hundred books, pamphlets and documents which he read in preparation for the work. Like *The Flying Years, Mine Inheritance* is a memorial to Niven's industry and integrity. But his determination to adhere closely to the record of history, his apparent reluctance to create an incident, however insignificant, or to introduce a character, however inconspicuous, not vouched for somewhere in the written annals of the Red River colony, are serious hindrances to the creation of a genuinely imaginative work of art. *Mine Inheritance* is neither fish nor flesh; it is not sober history and it is not imaginative fiction. It is not sober history because the incidents of history are presented subjectively and dramatically; and it is not imaginative fiction because Niven is reluctant to introduce material not warranted by the records of the colony, or to omit any which is.

The general pattern of *Mine Inheritance* is much the same as that of *The Flying Years*. The hero, David Baxter, comes to the Red River colony from Scotland; is employed as secretary to Miles Macdonell, the first governor of the colony; marries a beautiful half-breed girl, the daughter of a Scotch free-trader, who dies in childbirth; takes part ineffectively in the tragic affairs of the colony during its long struggle against the hostility of the Nor-Westers; remains in Red River during years of vicissitude and disappointment; marries Mari, a fine Scots lass who has always loved him and who is happy to rear Christina, the child of his first marriage; serves Miles Macdonell with a singleness of purpose which does more credit to his loyalty than his intelligence; and is made happy by the amalgamation of the North-West and Hudson's Bay companies, a union which for the colonists means the end of a long period of unrest and persecution and the beginning of a new and more tranquil era.

Niven's peculiar subservience to the facts of history as he saw them militates in several ways against the writing of an effective novel. As in *The Flying Years* his power of selection is again inadequate. He seems to be afraid to omit a single squabble between colonist and Nor-Wester, however trivial in action, however valueless in the illumination of character; so that most of the story is made up of scenes involving petty disputes, protests and counter-protests, heated and inconclusive argument, and — very occasionally — some violent action. Thus it is that when a really dramatic and tragic episode — the Seven Oaks massacre, for example — does figure in the narrative, its effectiveness is diminished because of the surrounding welter of petty detail.

Further, Niven's loyalty to the written record impedes him in the creation of characters in whom we can believe, and with whom we can at least partially sympathize. The Scots settlers of the Red River colony, in contrast to our traditional conception of the resolute, independent Highlandmen are, as depicted by Niven, a bloodless and miserable lot, ready to turn tail on the slightest provocation, incapable of defending themselves, longing only to return to the homeland. It is difficult to believe that such a group of colonists as Niven describes could have made a success of so difficult an undertaking as the establishment of a settlement in a new and hostile world. The leaders of the colony are worthy of their charge; they are vacillating and incompetent; and Niven's obvious sympathy and respect for Miles Macdonell, the first governor of the colony, cannot be shared by the reader. Niven does establish convincingly the magnitude of the difficulties which Macdonell faced; perhaps, we concede, he was not always vacillating and incompetent; but at best he follows the dictates of prudence and caution; and prudence and caution are not always the virtues which Niven apparently feels them to be, especially in the face of aggressive hostility.

A few of the minor characters of *Mine Inheritance* have life to the extent that they are able to enlist the active interest of the reader — men like MacDonald of Garth, a "king" of the North-West Company — like the Scots fur-trader and squawman, Court-Nez, "a mountain of a man . . . with a red glint in his eyes that were inclined to be peeping." But the hero, David Baxter, is never more than the shadow of a shadow, a dim bloodless figure serving with a kind of inhuman singleness of purpose a dim bloodless leader.

Like *The Flying Years, Mine Inheritance* is chiefly to be remembered because of the occasional passages which remind us that Frederick Niven was at times a poet. Where in Canadian literature, except perhaps elsewhere in Niven himself, is there more sensitive descriptive writing than this?

There was a sense of tranquility in the woods on either side — to some extent misleading, I knew, aware that the beasts in the recesses of the wilderness preyed one upon another. But there it was, that sense of tranquility, that ambient peace, something to remember for ever along with memories of that other, earlier, inland voyage from York Factory. There were swirls of water lit with green and orange reflections round wet-dark rocks; there were places where little lakes were strung like liquid sapphires through the wilderness, lake after lake. At night there were the owl-calls in cavernous forests; by day there were the plunging fish-hawks and the patient bunched herons standing on one leg. Out of the still woods on either side came the tapping of foraging wood-peckers.

Here was beauty enough, thought I, and why should anyone

have to die? Here was infinite peace, and why should people be at strife? The patter of rain on the leaves was even part of that sense of peace. Merganser and loon gave there the same cries that I had heard by Hayes River. There were polished green reaches on which lily leaves undulated in the ripples left by the canoes. There were slopes strewn with grey-blue granite boulders, and among the boulders grew berries in great clusters. There were stretches from which there was no foaming white escaping river to pole up or glide down, but only a reflection to paddle into and shatter. There were days of thunder-colour, purple woven in the forests, crashings and reverberations, windy lashings of water. Round a bend one day we came on a swim-ming moose and gave chase and it was shot as it lumbered up out of the shoaling water towards a slope of yellow pine — and so we had fresh moose-meat next day. There were sickle beaches on which the fine sand was like powdered ivory. On all sides was delight for the eye.

Under the stars we slipped past the North-West Company's Fort William, seeing only a light or two in its houses scattered along the bank and the twining reflections like snakes of gold in the water. The sequence of bay after bay, promontory after promontory of that vast inland sea of Lake Superior silenced me, the grey-blue granite, the seemingly interminable forest beyond.

IV

But in spite of the many passages of unusually fine descriptive writing, in spite of the occasional character creation who lives a little while in the reader's memory, what remains after a reading of Niven's novels of the Canadian West is chiefly an impression of unusual talents, of unmistakable sincerity of purpose, and of something gone seriously amiss. What is wrong with *The Flying Years* and *Mine Inheritance* is that the people in them do not live. And the extent of Niven's failure to give life to his characters is made clear by a com-parison between the Canadian novels and *Justice of the Peace,* the work which represents the high point of Niven's achieve-ment. In that fine novel there are two major characters, Mrs. Moir and her son Martin, and nearly a score of minor char-acters who live for a long time in the reader's memory. Moreover, although the book is lengthy it is never episodic; Niven's concentration on his theme, the destruction of a fine artist through a mother's jealous and unreasoning love, is altogether admirable, particularly since, in an account of an artist's life, there are numerous temptations to digression.

But *Justice of the Peace* was published in 1914; *The Flying Years* and *Mine Inheritance* quarter of a century later. It might be argued plausibly that quarter of a century is bound to affect, probably adversely, the quality of a man's imagination. This explanation of Niven's seeming loss of power in terms of the simple passing of time would be worth considering if we were able to find in *The Flying Years* and *Mine Inheritance* symptoms of the weariness which is a characteristic mark of work done under duress, when the creation of character and situation becomes an obvious and painful effort. But there are no such symptoms in either of these two novels. Rather, one is impressed by the author's seemingly inexhaustible energy, his determination to share with his reader every last scrap of his vast store of Western lore. Niven's enthusiasm is undiminished throughout; and he takes leave of his characters with obvious reluctance.

An investigation of the causes of Niven's comparative failure to write of the Canadian West in a manner worthy of his very great talents must therefore be concerned with something more complex than mere hardening of the arteries. The difference in artistic stature between *Justice of the Peace* and the novels which have their setting in the Canadian West raises the question: can a writer be a citizen of two countries? This is not of course a question of legal status, but one involving the human spirit. Does a native of one country ever write really well of another? Can a writer whose roots are deep in the soil of his native land — and paradoxically, roots sink deeper in the rocky soil of Scotland than almost anywhere else — ever be transplanted with complete success? In her autobiography, *Life and the Dream,* Mary Colum says of T. S. Eliot:

He must have been twenty-five or over when he settled in England, and that is really a rather late age for anyone educated in one continent to settle easily in another; that was my own age when I came to America and I realize it was a little too late for actual identification with American ways.

It is a fact that no Englishman brought up in his own country has ever written well of America; nor has any American — with the exception of Henry James — written well of England. Niven was a Scot by blood and education; and he did not settle in Canada until middle age. In these facts would seem to lie the true explanation of his inability to maintain the high level of artistry which he had reached comparatively early in life, while still in closest contact with his own land and people.

Niven knew Canada through books and through experience; but he knew Scotland because he was a part of it. It is here that we touch upon the fundamental difference between Niven's Scottish novels and those whose scenes are laid in the Canadian West. In *Ellen Adair, Justice of the Peace, The Staff at Simson's,* Niven moves through loved and familiar scenes, so loved and so familiar that he is able to suggest their peculiar character in a word which we feel to be exactly right. A man knowing another man well is able to characterize the other quickly and accurately because he knows what is important and what is irrelevant; but the man who knows little about another must tell all. There is in *Justice of the Peace* a striking and illuminating description of a Glasgow coffeehouse and certain other of Martin Moir's haunts in which surprisingly little attention is paid to specific and concrete detail. Rather, the description is highly suggestive; the essential outlines are sketched in quickly, the atmosphere conveyed by phrases rich in connotation:

Hurriedly would Martin return up Buchanan Street, hurriedly would he turn the corner at Edward's, hurriedly dash on to Ingram Street. Then suddenly he would disappear from the pavement as if swallowed up. He had indeed and in truth "run to earth." He had plunged down into the basement smoking-room of a tea-shop. There he ordered a cup of coffee and a cigarette. There he sat and dreamed on the broad and happy plush divan, while his heart returned to its normal beat. With a *Graphic* or a *London Illustrated News* on his knee he sat at rest, out of the odour of soft goods. He imagined himself slightly, vaguely in love with the girl in the little glass house upstairs, near the door, the cashier with the lustrous black hair. That added to the pleasure of fleeing, surreptitiously, from the unsought field of action. The visible world existed very acutely for him, and round him here, in Glasgow, he could match the pictures from many lands that he saw in the art journals at the Mitchell Library. Down in the smoke-room, the weeklies run through, he would ponder over his own unpainted pictures. Around Albion Street, and the Trongate, and in Wall Street, were such shops as Venice seemed to give to the etcher. There was a restaurant in Queen Street, where men stood to eat, a place that provided the most fascinating poses, quaint poses resembling the photographic-like ones in the illustrated weeklies. There was a public-house in Argyll Street, before the door of which wild girls in many petticoats, in high-heeled boots, with wild hair and tartan shawls over their heads, were always dancing and sparring and heel-and-toe shuffling like Steinlen figures. Beyond Kingston Dock — for he had wandered so far one lunch-hour instead of going to the Library, the day being too splendid to be cooped up — a day in which instead of saying "It is good to be alive!" one might well say "I believe I shall never die!" — wandering one day, looking at the river and the shipping, and the yelling stevedores dodging ropes and cranes, he found three or four little Spanish brigantines, with ear-ringed Iberians unloading oranges. Somehow a box broke, the oranges fell out, and the brown hands gathered up the golden fruit. The soft-goods warehouse was very far away.

In the Canadian novels there are some fine and moving descriptions of natural scenery; but those involving people contain none of the poetry of the wild girls in tartan shawls dancing and sparring and heel-and-toe shuffling like Steinlen figures, or of the ear-ringed Iberians gathering oranges in their brown hands. When Niven writes of his native land he writes of something that is a part of himself, and his scenes are sketched with the assurance that comes of knowing by instinct what is important. But when he writes of the Canadian scene that assurance vanishes; he relies on knowledge rather than feeling; and because he is not sure of what is important tends to crowd his canvas with unnecessary and distracting detail.

The truth is that after many years of residence in Canada Niven was still spiritually an alien, as perhaps all men must be who pass from one country to another comparatively late in life. Transplanting, to be successful, must be done early. Knowledge, enthusiasm, even love are not enough. If a writer is to suggest adequately the spirit of a region and its people he must himself be a part of that region. And Niven to the end of his life was a Scot.

But because he failed so measureably to live up to his true capabilities, because the divergence between what he attempted and what he accomplished is so marked, Niven has been underestimated in Canada. Indeed his most appreciative audience, for his Canadian as well as his Scottish novels, has always been in the Old Country. The truth is that in spite of his comparative failures he is much the most competent historical novelist to write of the Canadian West. No one can read *The Flying Years* and *Mine Inheritance* without reaching a greater understanding of the development of the West than most text-books are likely to give him. Perhaps some day a novelist will tell the story of the West in such a way as to bring to life the individuals who peopled the plains in the great days gone by. In the meantime we must be grateful to Frederick Niven for having given us work which, whatever its weaknesses, bears the stamp of integrity and craftsmanship.

The writer who seeks to inform his readers of the peculiar quality of a region such as the prairie provinces should be a pictorial artist able to describe accurately the physical features of a characteristic prairie landscape; he should be a poet with power to feel and to re-create imaginatively the particular atmosphere which invests the prairie scene; and lastly, he should be a psychologist with sufficient knowledge of human nature to be able to understand and describe the influence of the region upon the people who live within its confines. True regional literature is above all distinctive in that it illustrates the effect of particular, rather than general, physical, economic and racial features upon the lives of ordinary men and women. It should and usually does do many other things besides, but if it does not illustrate the influence of a limited and peculiar environment it is not true regional literature.

Among our Western Canadian writers there have been several — among whom Frederick Niven is outstanding — who have described adequately the physical characteristics of the prairie landscape; one or two, including W. O. Mitchell and Sinclair Ross, who have suggested with unusual sensitivity the peculiar atmosphere of the prairie region; but so far no one has indicated with more than partial success the subtle modifications of character which inevitably result from the influence upon ordinary men and women of a highly distinctive environment. The greatest single weakness of our Western writers is their inability to understand people in relation to their surroundings. Without such understanding the great novel of the prairies cannot be written.

II

Among Western writers Frederick Philip Grove seems to have seen more clearly than any other the responsibility of the writer who would give artistic expression to a distinctive regional spirit. He at least never minimized the magnitude of the task nor the probability of failure. In his autobiography, *In Search of Myself,* he recalls a self-evaluation made in 1912 when he paused for a moment at middle age to ponder what he might do in the future:

Meanwhile there was, in this casting-up of accounts, one thing which stood on the asset side, against much which I must necessarily put down in the list of liabilities. The one asset consisted in this: that I could truthfully call my knowledge of the pioneering section of the west of the North American continent unique. At a glance I could survey the prairie country from Kansas to Saskatchewan or Alberta; and at a thought I could evaluate, in my own way of course, the implications of pioneer life. I, the cosmopolitan, had fitted myself to be the spokesman of a race — not necessarily a race in the ethnographic sense; in fact, not at all in that sense; rather in the sense of a stratum of society which cross-sectioned all races, consisting of those who, in no matter what climate, at no matter what time, feel the impulse of starting anew, from the ground up, to fashion a new world which might serve as the breeding place of a civilization to come. These people, the pioneers, reaffirmed me in my conception of what often takes the form of a tragic experience; the age-old conflict between human desire and the stubborn resistance of nature. Order must arise out of chaos; the wilderness must be tamed. No matter where I looked, then as today, I failed to see that the task of recording that struggle with nature had ever adequately been done, not even by Hamsun, who, for the sake of a pleasant ending, gave, to Isaak, Geissler. To record that struggle seemed to be my task. Perhaps, very likely even, I was foredoomed to failure in my endeavour; in fact, I seemed to see even then that I was bound to fail; but the attempt had to be made.

The premonition of failure here suggested was not the consequence of ordinary lack of confidence. Grove never underestimated his own powers. Indeed it is a serious weakness in him that he never seems to have been aware of the uncertainties of technique which mar much of his work and which humble self-appraisal might have done something to remedy. Rather, he felt that the petty necessity of earning his bread and butter prevented him from achieving the detachment which the great artist must have if he is to preserve his spiritual integrity:

In the last analysis it all came down to an economic problem. In order to see things once more from the outside, I must regain my distance; in order to regain my distance I must, economically and otherwise, get away from my present milieu.

But Grove was never permitted to escape from his "present milieu." It was his fate to be harassed all his life by the grimmest kind of economic necessity. None the less, the attempt to record adequately the "age-old conflict between human desire and the stubborn resistance of nature" was made. That attempt, as Grove had anticipated, failed. But the causes of failure lie not so much in the physical circumstances surrounding the act of creation, as Grove himself seems inclined to believe, as in his incomplete understanding of men and women.

Grove's story of man's struggle against the stubborn resistance of nature is localized in a Western Canadian setting in four of his novels, *Settlers of the Marsh* (1925); *Our Daily Bread* (1928); *The Yoke of Life* (1930); and *Fruits of the Earth* (1933). These four novels, published when Grove was well past middle age, together with two collections of descriptive essays, *Over Prairie Trails* (1922); and *The Turn of the Year* (1923), constitute the most considerable attempt yet made to describe the Western Canadian scene and to chronicle the lives of the people living within its borders. But in spite of Grove's avowed purpose, in none of the four novels is "the age-old conflict between human desire and the stubborn resistance of nature" the real centre of interest. John Elliott of *Our Daily Bread* and Abe Spaulding of *Fruits of the Earth* are both resolute men who dream of owning vast tracts of land, not so much for the wealth inherent in possession as for the satisfaction of an obscure desire for power and permanency. The will to take roots is strong in both John Elliott and Abe Spaulding, as it is in most men. The land itself, rather than its fruits, is what matters. But the struggle of the hero to conquer the land is not of paramount interest in either novel; the real battle is that of man against man, warfare that is never openly declared and which is really a clash between naturally conflicting rather than deliberately hostile forces. Such a struggle is inherently far more dramatic than one between man and his physical environment, as Grove clearly realized. Thus it is that in *Our Daily Bread* John Elliott's fight to establish himself as a wealthy landowner is over before the story which Grove has to tell begins. When we meet Elliott in the opening pages he is fifty-five years old; and the story of his conquest of the land is told in a paragraph. In *Fruits of the Earth* the hero, Abe Spaulding, begins, it is true, from scratch; but it is obvious after the first few pages that he is destined to succeed in a material way; and the reader has at no time the feeling that he is witnessing a conflict of which the outcome is doubtful; indeed, he is almost certain to be bored by the repetitious examples of Abe's shrewdness and foresight. The struggle of man, personified in Abe Spaulding, against nature, is easy, the outcome certain, and hence the dramatic interest inconsequential.

It is possible that had Grove concentrated to a greater degree than he did on the struggle of man to conquer nature — and this after all was his declared theme — his work might have been better than it is. But he was diverted into writing of a struggle even more dramatic — that between a man and his own flesh and blood — but for which he had limited talent. It is of course a kind of conflict which may be related to the struggle between man and his physical environment, since it is a natural development of that transitional stage of pioneer life when old and new inevitably clash; but Grove's knowledge of human nature was not, unfortunately, as broad or as deep as his knowledge of physical environment.

The conflict in both *Our Daily Bread* and *Fruits of the Earth* is as old as the race — man against his own flesh and blood, the father against his children. John Elliott and Abe

Spaulding are patriarchal types; anachronisms in their time, but not completely out of harmony with their environment, for the great agricultural and pastoral regions of the earth have always fostered the patriarchal way of life. To John Elliott it is a sin against nature that children should grow away from their parents and seek to lead independent lives; and the fact that his own children seek to escape his authority, and eventually do so, is the tragedy that darkens his declining years. In the same way Abe Spaulding is concerned because his children grow away from him and the farm, attracted by the tawdry glitter of small-town life. But Abe is a stronger man than John Elliott, and a good deal less sensitive and introspective. In the end he reasserts a measure of authority over family and community and so gains a victory in which neither he nor the reader can take much pleasure.

Grove's failure is not one of judgment. The conflict between father and child is a magnificent theme of tragedy admitting of endless variation; but Grove is unable to make us feel that the situation as he describes it *is* tragic. John Elliott more often than not appears to be a selfish man of few inner resources whose desire to dominate his family removes him from the range of the reader's sympathy; hence in defeat he is not a tragic but merely a pathetic figure. Nor is it possible to feel much concern about the fate of the rebellious children, who are so devoid of life as to be incapable of arousing in the reader emotions of love or hate or even of interest. The Elliotts are a large family; but the members are without discernible individuality.

It is unfortunate that Grove was unable to create characters capable of sustaining his theme, because his conception of the theme itself is a noble one. This conception is embodied in a passage which expresses John Elliott's attitude towards his life on the land, and towards his children who deny the validity of that attitude:

Through all his activities, then, a single purpose had run: the purpose of honourably raising his family, a large family at that. His favourite story from the Bible had been that of Abraham and his house; often had he repeated to himself the lines, "In blessing I will bless thee; and in multiplying I will multiply thy seed as the stars of the heaven and as the sand which is upon the sea-shore. And in thy seed shall all the nations of the earth be blessed.''

Never had he, in these lines, seen or sought for evidence of verbal revelation; purely theological thought had been unknown to him. He had taken them simply as an expression of the marvel of fruitful propagation.

That single purpose had co-ordinated all things for him, had justified them; had seemed to transform his whole life with all its ramifications into a single, organic whole with a clear and unmistakable meaning. In that purpose he and his wife had been one; and so they had been fruitful and multiplied. It was the children's duty to conform, to become like them; and therefore, to obey them in all things, so as to multiply the seed themselves one day; so as not to let the strand thus created perish. To live honourably, to till the land, and to hand on life from generation to generation; that was man's duty; that, to him, in spite of all doubts, had meant and still meant serving God. Doubt had existed only as to details; it had never gnawed at the root of the fundamentals. . . .

Empires rose and fell; kings and high priests strove with each other; wars were fought; ripples on the sea of life. Underneath, deep down, that life itself went on as it had done in Abraham's time: the land was tilled to grow our daily bread. And this life, the life of the vast majority of men on earth, was the essential life of all mankind. The city with its multifarious activities was nothing but a bubble on that sea.

He was proud of belonging to the hidden groundmass of that race which carried on essential tasks, no matter under what form of government, no matter under what conditions of climate and soil: he had lived and multiplied; he had grown, created, not *acquired* his and his children's daily bread: he had served God.

There are fewer nobler meditations on the dignity and greatness of the farmer's way of life than this. As in Hardy's *In Time of the Breaking of Nations* there is recognition of the mystical significance of the tilling of the soil, an awareness of labour which is part of a religious ceremony although the participant in the ceremony may have no physical feeling beyond that of fatigue and no emotion beyond hope of gain. And Grove, in articulating John Elliott's bitterness when he sees his family scatter from him, expresses admirably the emotion of the instinctive patriarch who at the end of his life finds himself abandoned by those whom he created expressly to carry on his work:

> He had failed in the achievement of the second dream of his life. Half the purpose of his whole existence was gone. His children were scattered over two provinces of this country: they had freed themselves from the paternal rule: they were rebels in the house of their father: their aims were not what his had been. Their lives were evil; their lives were chaos; and through their lives, his own was chaos.

Here then, is a lofty theme, loftily uttered. But John Elliott never rises to the heights of tragic dignity which the theme demands. He is more often than not a petty, irritable old man who makes little attempt to understand his children, who resents their going from him without ever giving them much reason to wish to do otherwise. "Lear of the prairies" one of his more literate acquaintances calls him; and it is true that as Lear his creator visualized him. But the description is utterly inept. Lear is a Titan, the central figure in a struggle waged by the forces of good and evil in the awful forms of his own children. But the young Elliotts inspire no awe; and scarcely any other emotion. They are negligible. So it is that old John Elliott crawls towards death, an abandoned and pathetic figure certainly, but about whom it is impossible to feel great anger or great grief. Too much of the time he and his family are little more than shadowy symbols, so far removed from the tremendous flesh and blood creations which surround Shakespeare's king as to make comparison a mockery.

Grove's failure in *Our Daily Bread* is chiefly a failure in comprehension. But his technique is also stumbling and uncertain. The narrative is episodic; and the steps in John Elliott's physical and spiritual breakdown are often indicated rather than described. Thus it is that we are sometimes confronted with a John Elliott years older and infinitely more embittered than the John Elliott of the preceding chapter. The force of V. S. Pritchett's dictum that it is less the business of the novelist to tell us what happened than to show us how it happened is illustrated, in a negative way, by Grove's failure to discuss fully the successive steps in John Elliott's decline and fall. We are compelled to take on faith what the artist should have dramatized for us; and our faith is not always strong enough.

III

The theme of *Our Daily Bread* is repeated with some variation in *Fruits of the Earth*. But Abe Spaulding is a stronger character than John Elliott. Grove seems to have seen more clearly than in any of his earlier novels just what he wanted to make of his hero and to have gone about his task with considerable assurance. Like Elliott, Abe Spaulding is an instinctive patriarch whose dream it is to own many acres of land and to be the father of many children who will care for the land after him. He homesteads in the marsh lands of Manitoba, is assisted at all times by that faculty of shrewd judgment without which even the hardest labour is likely to go unrewarded, and is soon recognized as the most important community citizen and a natural leader of men. But because Abe, like John Elliott, is a patriarch born out of due time, he and his family tend to grow apart. Between him and his wife and children there is little understanding, little sympathy. The great tragedy of Abe's life, in terms of a single incident, is the death of his young son Charlie, a dreamy sensitive youngster whom, rather illogically, Abe loves far more than he does any of his other three children. It is an irony probably quite unpremeditated on Grove's part that we are made to feel the inevitability of the favourite son, had he lived, being of all the children the least in sympathy with his father's ideals.

Spaulding's re-emergence, in the last chapter or two of the book, as the community leader and strong man, is unconvincing. In spite of Grove's insistence that Spaulding's morality is that of the majority of the settlers, that what he does is what "in a similar situation nine hundred and ninety-nine men out of a thousand would have done if they had dared," the reader is likely to have the uneasy feeling that he is witnessing the petty and temporary triumph of one who is not the local Hampden that his creator intended him to be.

The great weakness of *Fruits of the Earth,* considered not

as a social document but as a work of art, is up to a point the weakness of *Our Daily Bread*. The people are names and little else besides. The daughters of Abe Spaulding are not clearly distinguished from one another; and none of the score or more of minor characters who figure in the chronicle has sufficient personality to fix him for any length of time in the reader's mind. Nor indeed has Abe Spaulding himself. But the fact that he is less a human being than a symbol is by design of his creator. For Abe Spaulding is intended to be something more than an ordinary human being. It is no fault of Grove's design, but of his execution, that Spaulding ends by being something less. In his autobiography, *In Search of Myself*, Grove gives us an account of the genesis of his hero. On his way to town across the open prairie with a load of grain, he saw one day far off on the crest of a hill, looking like a giant against the sunset, a man ploughing. The ploughman was the first human being Grove had seen in that part of the country. Grove spoke to him, and immediately regretted having done so. Too close association dispelled the magic of that first spectacular appearance against the flaming sunset:

Already, while he was standing by the side of the trail, with me reclining on top of my load of a hundred bushels of wheat; and more especially when he had uttered the last few words, he had not seemed to me to be quite the sort of giant I had imagined when he had first topped the crest of the hill. Yet, somehow, he had boded forth for me the essence of the pioneering spirit which has settled the vast western plains and with which I had, through scores of concrete manifestations, become familiar during the preceding year.

The important thing was this. His first appearance, on top of the hill, had tripped a trigger in my imagination; he had become one with many others I had known; and an explosion had followed it in the nerve-centres of my brain because I had been ready for it. I had, for some time, been ready for the pains of birth. A, to me, momentous thing had happened; the figure of Abe Spaulding, central to the book which, forty years later, was published under the title, *Fruits of the Earth*, had been born in my mind, fully armed as it were, and focalizing in itself a hundred features which I had noticed elsewhere. This man, this giant in body, if not mind and spirit, had furnished the physical features for a vision which had, so far, been incomplete because it had been abstract.

If I had seen the entirely casual occasion — that is all I can call him; he was not the prototype — of this figure again, if I had heard him speak as no doubt he had been used to speak, without relevance to my creation, that mental vision of mine would have been profoundly disturbed. A perfectly irrelevant actuality would have been superimposed upon my conception of a man who, as I saw him, had perhaps never lived; for he lacked that infusion of myself which makes him what he has become. From a type and a symbol, he would have become an individual; he would have been drained of the truth that lived in him; he would have become a mere fact.

This passage suggests Grove's power and his limitations. His view of man is philosophic; but in order to impose his view upon his readers he is impelled to see man not as an individual but as a symbol; and symbols, no matter how ingeniously created, are in the end lifeless things. Abe Spaulding and John Elliott symbolize the patriarchal outlook. And that infusion of himself, which Grove says exists in Abe Spaulding, is wholly inadequate to give reality to figures who in primary conception are intended to embody a view of life, rather than to *be* life itself.

This tendency to make his characters symbols rather than human beings is apparent in Grove's two novels which deal with settlement life in the northern Manitoba bush country. We are willing to accept Grove's statement that he actually knew a man so naive in sexual matters that up to the day of his marriage he had not known of the essential difference between male and female. But the fact that such a man may exist does not necessarily make him an acceptable hero of a novel. And Grove is not equal to the task which he sets himself in *Settlers of the Marsh* — that of making the central character, Niels Lindstedt, believable.

The hero of *The Yoke of Life,* Len Sterner, is for a time a recognizable human being, a frustrated farm boy seeking escape through education from a way of life which he finds repellent. But he too, becomes a symbol — of the ascetic spirit in a fleshly world — and the struggle between instinctive purity and sexual desire has little meaning because the protagonists, Len and Lydia, have almost nothing in common with recognizable human beings. Len's inhuman and hence unconvincing triumph through death is described in lofty and mystical terms; but the language of the philosopher is inadequate to make real the behaviour of beings remote from flesh and blood.

Because of his temperament Grove could never have been a great novelist. His autobiography, *In Search of Myself,* is the story of a man who, whatever his physical experiences, lived remote from the centre of life. He views his fellow men intellectually, never emotionally. He is a lonely, ascetic figure, repelled rather than attracted by humanity. A reading of *In Search of Myself,* serves to confirm one of the strongest impressions left by the novels, that Grove rarely, if ever, felt warmly towards any human being. Partly this impression may result from a horror on Grove's part of any kind of emotional display; but one is compelled to suspect, as in the case of his hero Len Sterner, an almost pathological shrinking from the animal that is man.

It is never enough that the novelist understand fully the technique of his art, or that he have the power to describe exciting incidents in vivid terms, or that he have a philosophical view of life which he expounds with eloquence; he must, above all else, know people intimately and be able to bring them to life in his pages. It is not possible to quarrel seriously with Virginia Woolf's assertion that all novels "deal with character, and that it is to express character, not to preach doctrines, sing songs, or celebrate the glories of the British Empire, that the form of the novel, so clumsy, verbose and undramatic, so rich, elastic and alive, has been evolved." But Grove's people are only occasionally human beings; the main figures are shadowy symbols around whom gather swarms of puppets — the Elliotts and the Spauldings, and the neighbours who are seldom anything more than names, and occasionally grotesques like Mr. Pennycup and Mr. Suddaby and John Elliott, Junior, who live awhile in the memory because their remoteness from reality startles us into looking at them twice.

Grove's lack of sympathetic understanding of his fellow man is most obvious in his inability to reproduce with even a measurable degree of accuracy the ordinary conversation of ordinary people. Who can imagine any farm-boy — even one who loves literature — speaking, under stress of great emotion, as Len Sterner speaks to Lydia?

At last Len spoke. He did not look at her as he did so; he was intent only on finding the exact expression for the change which he had observed. His words seemed hardly to be addressed to her.

"Under the eaves of our sheep-shed," he said, "there hangs a pupa, attached to the boards by a fine, thin stalk. It is greyish brown and quite plain. It looks like the wood and has been there since last fall. Inside of it something is growing; and soon it will burst its shell. It will be a butterfly, checkered in gold and black. . . ."

His head moved and he looked full into her eyes. Little ripples of expectation ran along her spine. And then the bubble burst, precipitating her into a strange confusion of feelings.

"That is you," he said. "While you were at home you were the pupa. You have burst your shell and become a butterfly."

Or again, it is possible to conceive of any girl writing such a letter as Dr. Vanbruik shows to Abe Spaulding, even after making all possible allowance for the extravagances of the jazz age?

My dear Vi, — Oh boy! I'm all tipsy and raring to go. Oh kid! Ma has relented. I'm going to attend a swell dance tomorrow night where the Tip Top Orchestra is playing. My togs are ready, compact filled, hair frizzed and all. Of course, Ma doesn't know; but Jack will be there with bells on. She thinks he's at Torquay yet. But this once I'm going to have a fling. Dash it, though! I was mad at Jack the other day, a week ago. You know that nifty compact he gave me last Xmas? He smashed it; and I gave him Hail Columbia. He'll bring me a new one tomorrow night; that'll be jake with me. Didn't I feel punk though!

Last night I met Agnes Strong on the ice. For the love of Pete! How that Jane carries on! I'd be ashamed of myself, honest to cats I would. You know Frank Smith the new shiek? He's sweet on me; and of course, I encourage him. Want some fun. But Agnes is cuckooed about him since he took her to a dance last week. It makes me puke to see her. Well, so long kiddo. Must ring off. Think of me tomorrow night, all dolled up. Frank says I'm a spiff looker. Hug me tight. See you in the funnies! — Pansy Blossom.

Here, unmistakably, one gets the impression of the author painstakingly gathering together a score of slang phrases, all of them popular in the early twenties, and weaving them together into a mosaic which, while containing not a word unsanctified by current usage has in its totality nothing whatever in common with the way in which the youngsters of the jazz age expressed themselves. It is necessary only to compare the manner in which Ring Lardner handles the slang of the same period to comprehend the difference in artistic achievement between one whose knowledge of current jargon is academic and one who knows it through intimate acquaintance with those who create and speak it.

IV

But although Grove is not a great novelist there are some things in his writing which are memorable. The tragedy of his artistic life is that so much of his work was done in a medium for which he had little talent. His best bits of writing are descriptive and philosophical rather than narrative. In a milieu less harassing it is possible that he might have been a distinguished essayist. He has a keen eye and the power to record accurately what he sees. There are, too, some fine passages of philosophic meditation in the novels, such as the reflection, in *Our Daily Bread,* on the farmer's way of life; and in the same book, the sombre moving soliloquy on death expressed in the form of the thoughts which pass through John Elliott's mind as he sits by the bedside of his dying son-in-law, which do much to make the banal dialogue and inadequately realized characterization tolerable. But it is not possible to read Grove's two collections of descriptive pieces, *Over Prairie Trails* and *The Turn of the Year,* without feeling that his best work lies in just such things as these. In them he is able to combine an accurate eye for description and the philosophic strain so strong in him without impeding the development of plot or characterization. The pity of it is that Grove, either because of economic pressure or a mistaken estimate of his own powers, felt impelled to work in a medium which was not suited to his peculiar talents.

Not that we would willingly give up any of the novels of the Canadian West which Grove wrote. Imperfect though they are they reflect a maturity of intellect lacking in most of our fiction. Grove is not a great novelist, for the power to create living people was denied him; but he brought a cultured and philosophic mind to the contemplation of the Western scene, and an eye for specific detail which will make his work a valuable source of information to the rural historian of the future. His statement of purpose in writing *Fruits of the Earth* — "to infuse a dramatic interest into agricultural operations and that attendant rural life thereof" — holds true of all his Western novels. He failed to infuse adequately the dramatic interest, but his record of "agricultural operations and the attendant rural life thereof" is one of the most accurate in Canadian fiction.

In Western Canada there is to be seen today that most fascinating of all human phenomena, the making of a nation. Out of
breeds diverse in traditions, in ideals, in speech, and in manner
of life, Saxon and Slav, Teuton, Celt and Gaul, one people is
being made. The blood strains of great races will mingle in the
blood of a race greater than the greatest of them all.

Thus Ralph Connor in typically idealistic and prophetic
strain, indirectly calling attention to what would seem to be
for the novelist a theme, founded on conflict and reconciliation, that is rich in dramatic possibilities. Certainly the clash,
and ultimately the merging, of alien cultures, has nowhere
else in Canada been more clearly observable than on the
prairies. In the last decades of the nineteenth century and the
first of the twentieth the Canadian west was, to the ambitious,
the poor, the persecuted of a score of European countries, a
land rich in all things the unsatisfied heart craved for, a land
untainted by the sins and cruelties and exploitations of a
hundred generations, a clean naked land where a man might
make his own way in his own way, rear his family, worship his
gods, cherish the customs of his fathers while evading their
oppressions, and live in peace with his fellow men.

Such was the dream. In some instances, perhaps most, it was
in a measure realized; but what the dreamers, the idealists
overlooked was the hard fact that while the land itself might
be new and untainted and fair, the men who settled it were
creatures of Adam who carried their birthright with them.

They earned their bread — a small loaf it often was — by the sweat of their brow; they quarrelled bitterly with their neighbours who were of different tongue and blood; they hated the tax collector who took from them what they believed they had legitimately earned for themselves, and they protested government laws which compelled them to support schools where children were taught in a language not their own. Ultimately, and most bitterly of all, many of the original settlers fought with their own children of the second and third generations who chose to deny the tongue and customs of their forefathers, seeking to be known, and legitimately so, not as Ukrainian or Pole or Icelander or Dane but quite simply Canadian.

There was yet another basic conflict to be resolved in the painful process of nation-making — this between the Anglo-Saxon would-be overlord and the (in his eyes) lesser breeds who spoke not the Queen's tongue and wore no Old School Tie. (In most instances no tie at all.) This determination of the part of the Anglo-Saxon, and most specifically the Englishman, to establish the superiority and preserve the integrity of his race manifested itself primarily in two ways — through deliberate segregation in tightly-knit insulated colonies, and through active propagandizing for the imposition of severe restrictions on immigration from countries other than Great Britain. The first of these techniques of self-preservation led to the emerging of tight little islands of Englishmen here and there on the prairie ocean — communities such as Cannington Manor in Saskatchewan where men and women of undefiled blood rode to hounds (in pursuit of jackrabbits and coyotes), played cricket and tennis on the gopherhole-pocked prairie, drank tea every afternoon at the traditional hour and worshipped every Sunday in the little Anglican church which was at once a place of spiritual refreshment and a symbol of Imperial solidarity. Inevitably these attempts of the Anglo-Saxon to live uncontaminated by contact with his alleged inferiors were frustrated by the realities of the pioneer way of life. Survival in a pioneer society has always been in part dependent on co-operation with one's neighbour, a lesson that even the most insular Old Country man was quickly compelled to learn. Then too, the attitude of that neighbour, were he German or Swede or Russian or Pole or Hungarian, made the preservation of a sense of racial superiority difficult. Far from humbling himself in the presence of the Britisher the "foreigner" as often as not condescended to him by reason of his own superior farming skills.

Surprisingly, since most of their members were highly literate, very little has been written about these curious colonies which during the brief period of their flourishing must be credited with providing a wealth of comic relief from the generally serious problems of survival in a new harsh land. Harold Bindloss, a prolific English novelist unsympathetic to the pretensions of his colonizing countrymen, touched on the theme of prairie Imperialism in several of his novels and at some length in *The Frontiersman* (1908); but the most significant cultural consequence of the segregated Old Country settlement has been the creation of a vast store of "green Englishman" stories, many of which are still to be heard wherever western old-timers foregather.

Of the few books depicting the struggles of the British to survive intact in a hostile environment (pride at first inhibiting them from accepting the advice and assistance of knowledgeable would-be neighbours) the most readable is Harry Pick's *Next Year* (1928), which deals with the founding of the Barr Colony in that part of the West now centered on the town of Lloydminster. The fictional form which the author — himself a Barr Colonist — employs, is, however, little more than a convenient device to allow him certain freedoms which the direct autobiographical approach might inhibit.

The efforts of true-blue Britishers to restrict immigration into Canada from foreign lands are reflected in books, pamphlets and letters to the press which were published in surprising numbers during the early decades of our century. An excerpt from a book written about the Barr Colony by one of the colonists, Colonel J. Hanna McCormick, expounds the thesis and suggests the general tone of these publications: "As a notable result [of the existing immigration policy] take the lamentable strike in Winnipeg, and the attempt to foist a Soviet government on the city. A serious state of affairs prevailed there for some time, whilst Montreal, Vancouver, Calgary and other parts affected, watched developments in order to come in once this initial attempt was successful. So, these people being here — haters of law and order — what secret and dark work might not be hatched!" Although Colonel McCormick detected a bomb-made bulge in the breast-pocket of every Slav immigrant, he was prepared to tolerate aliens in the country for the time being, providing their number was not added to. They were, after all, a valuable source of cheap labour. "As to shipping aliens out of the country, lock stock and barrel, for humane motives this is not possible in the present state of a half-starved Europe. In the aggregate there are a few millions thus to be disposed of, and Canada requires their labour, since British emigration is in the re-arranging state owing to lack of transportation."

All this as late as 1923.

II

Ralph Connor was fully aware of the intense hostility felt by many of his own blood and race towards men of alien lands, and lent his talents and considerable moral influence to the task of counteracting the pressures generated by the Keep-Canada-British propagandists. "It would be our wisdom," he wrote, "to grip these peoples to us with living hooks of justice and charity till all lines of national cleavage disappear, and in the Entity of our Canadian national life, and in the Unity of our world-wide Empire, we fuse into a people whose strength will endure the slow shock of time for the honour of our name, for the good of mankind, and for the glory of Almighty God."

Ralph Connor was himself the first writer to see clearly the dramatic potential of the nation-building theme and to exploit this potential in fictional form. Characteristically *The Foreigner,* published in 1909, combines melodrama with a direct appeal for a sympathetic appreciation of the foreigner and his ways. The set pieces of description which record the activities of first-generation central Europeans herded together in the city of Winnipeg, struggling to make a living in a new world and at the same time to perpetuate the folkways of the old are done with sympathy and understanding based on acute observation and instinctive Christian charity:

Close to the railway tracks and in the more unfashionable northern section of the little city a huddling cluster of little shacks gave a central European colony shelter. With a sprinkling of Germans, Italians and Swiss, it was almost solidly Slav. Slavs of all varieties from all provinces and speaking all dialects were there to be found. Slavs from Little Russia and from Great Russia, the alert Polack, the heavy Croatian, the haughty Magyar, and occasionally the stalwart Dalmatian from the Adriatic, in speech mostly Ruthenian, in religion orthodox Greek Catholic or Uniat and Roman Catholic. By their non-discriminating Anglo-Saxon fellow-citizens they are called Galacians, or by the unlearned, with an echo of parts of Paul's Epistle in their minds, 'Galatians'. There they pack together in their little shacks of boards and tar-paper, with pent roofs of old tobacco tins or of slabs of that same useful but unsightly tar-paper, crowding each other in close irregular groups as if the whole wide prairies were not there inviting them. From the number of their huts they seem a colony of no great size, but the census taker, counting ten or twenty to a hut, is surprised to find them run into hundreds. During the summer months they are found far away in the colonies of their kinsfolk, here and there planted upon the prairies, or out in gangs where new lines of railway are in construction, the joy of the contractor's heart, glad to exchange their steady uncomplaining toil for the uncertain spasmodic labour of their English-speaking rivals. But winter finds them once more crowding back into the little black shacks in the foreign quarter of the city, drawn thither by their traditional social instincts, or driven by economic necessities. All they ask is bed space on the floor or, for a higher price, on the home-made bunks that line the walls, and a woman to cook the food they bring her; or failing such a happy arrangement, a stove on which they may boil their varied stews of beans or barley, beets or rice or cabbage, with such scraps of pork or beef from the neck or flank as they can beg or buy at low price from the slaughter houses.

It is from such an environment that Ralph Connor's hero emerges to win the heart and hand of a beautiful Anglo-Saxon girl — no less than the daughter of a peer. It need hardly be said that the hero is assisted in his spectacular rise by several stock Ralph Connor characters — the well-educated and ultimately reformed alcoholic, the dedicated missionary, and of course the pure-hearted gorgeous golden girl who is Mary Robertson in yet another of her numerous guises.

The activities of a bomb-throwing Russian nihilist do, however, introduce a new and explosive note into western Canadian fiction.

For all its traditionally happy ending *The Foreigner* is a sombre book, too unpleasantly realistic to suit the romantic tastes of the average novel-reader of the period. In point of sales it marked the beginning of the decline of Ralph Connor's popularity — ironically so, because in spite of its manifest absurdities *The Foreigner* is a much more convincing artistic achievement than several of Ralph Connor's immense popular successes — notably *The Doctor* and *The Prospector* — that preceded it.

III

The most popular novel in Canadian literature based on a mass migration movement is Laura Goodman Salverson's *The Viking Heart* (1923). Mrs. Salverson (1890-   ) was herself the daughter of Icelanders who came to Canada in the 1870's, and her memories of childhood embraced stories told her by her parents of the hardships endured by the early settlers. Of necessity Mrs. Salverson traces, within the limits of her fictional framework, the fortunes of only a few Icelandic families who came to northern Manitoba following the disastrous volcanic eruptions of 1876 in their homeland. But the families are sufficiently varied to constitute a fairly representative cross-section of the Icelandic community of Gimli, and their struggles are common to most of the immigrants of the period.

The great popularity of *The Viking Heart* is of a most satisfying kind; it is deserved, and it is easy to account for. Mrs. Salverson, like so many Westerners in the decades prior to the thirties, is a romantic optimist. Her romanticism is evident in the opening pages of the novel, when she dreams of her ancestors much as the exiled Celt dreams of the green hills of Erin or the lone sheiling on the misty island; and the picture she paints of Icelandic home-life, so soon to be destroyed by volcanic eruption, has the quiet charm of a pastoral idyll. The immigrants' first glimpse of a native of the New World is also described in conventionally romantic terms:

As the sun set, bathing the river in crimson and amber glory, casting a ghostly glimmer over the ragged autumn woods on either side, there flashed into sight from beyond a bend in the river a craft, long and slender, cleaving the water with the swiftness and silence of thought. And the foreigners from the far north country saw their first red man. A splendid native, straight and supple, like some bronze god baring his copper chest indifferent to the elements, he bore down on them. For one fleeting moment he appeared as if painted against the crimson sky, then rounding the bend drifted into the shadows of the farther shore.

The Icelanders encounter hardships without precedent in their own lives or the lives of their ancestors of many generations, but their sufferings leave no permanent scars. As we follow the fortunes of Bjorn and Borga Lindal, the young couple who fall in love on the way to the colony and are married a year or two later, we sense that no matter what trials may befall them their eventual triumphs, both material and spiritual, are inevitable. So we read in the comfortable assurance that everything is going to turn out all right in the end; and at the same time fall victims to the illusion of reality which Mrs. Salverson with considerable skill creates.

For the seeming reality of this tale of Icelandic settlement is indeed at many points an illusion created in part through frequent reference to and tentative discussion of the innumerable problems which beset a people trying to establish themselves in a new world. But Mrs. Salverson never gets beyond the point of tentative discussion. We are told that Bjorn and Borga worked very hard and met with many disappointments; but in the tale itself their trials are passed over so lightly that they make little or no impression on us. Even when the Lindals' crop is completely hailed out and it seems that the boy Thor will be balked of his ambition to go to college and study medicine, the tragedy is of short duration. In a manner reminiscent of the fairy godmother, Elizabeth, the elder daughter of the family, produces her store of secret savings — more than enough to send Thor to college — and all is sunshine again. A hailstorm which has utterly destroyed a year's work is thus made an excuse to play a delightful surprise on the reader. And even when tragedy strikes in its decisive form and Thor, the beloved son, dies in battle, the blow is softened for the family by the birth, shortly afterwards, of a Lindal grandson, Thor the second.

The story of Anna and Loki Fjalsted, neighbours of the Lindals, is for a time told on the level of deeply-moving tragedy; and the gentle, sensitive Anna's complete mental breakdown when her brutal husband compels her to hold a pail to catch the blood that spurts from the throat of the calf he is butchering, is described with convincing realism. But the pity and the terror are not sustained. Anna becomes a queer woodland faun who sings strange songs in a voice of haunting beauty; Loki, the husband, repents of his brutal ways; and the son Balder grows up to be a great musician who achieves success with astonishing ease. And when Loki dies, Anna's faculties are miraculously restored to her.

All this of course is the elementary stuff of romance. It is impossible not to feel that Mrs. Salverson has largely ignored most of the main problems of prairie settlement insofar as they are related to character, although she does go so far as to state one of these problems through the words of Bjorn Lindal:

Bjorn nodded soberly, then he said, "When I remember the wild plans I had in youth for gaining recognition and position after a few years in this country, it seems a huge joke. You know the attitude that the people had towards us. Suspicion, distrust, contempt. A little of that faded when we proved our worth in the rebellion — it has never been said, or ever will, I hope, that a Norseman can't defend his home. But we Icelanders are still a curiosity to many. They think us creatures of doubtful habit and uncertain intelligence. They tolerate us because we are useful — because we are doing what they refuse to do, being of such superior clay.

But the problem, thus stated, is never dramatized. Of the hostility of the old established settler, and most specifically the Anglo-Saxon settler, to the newcomer — and it is a reality in almost every community in the West, and indeed wherever an alien goes — we hear and see nothing more.

Although *The Viking Heart* is not, as has so often been claimed for it, a serious realistic treatment of Icelandic settlement in Manitoba, it is a fine romantic tale, written with much sympathy and understanding and tenderness and love. The characters are the creatures of romance, but they are vividly drawn. Perhaps Elizabeth is a little too good and her sister Ninna a little too heartless to ring entirely true, but they are at times very much alive. And although Balder's awakening, when Ninna marries a rich contractor, to the realization that it was really Elizabeth whom he had loved all the time, is hardly the stuff of life as we know it, it fits perfectly into the story which Mrs. Salverson has to tell.

There is about *The Viking Heart* a beguiling sunlit charm which fully justifies its popularity. Mrs. Salverson idealizes her people; but she does so with such conviction that she almost persuades us of the existence of persons like the Lindals and Halssons and Balder Fjalsted. And that we do believe in them, if only for the time of reading, is proof of the skill with which they have been created.

None of Mrs. Salverson's later novels has measured up to the standard of *The Viking Heart*. Her historical tales are exotic and unconvincing, and her handling of theme in *The Dark Weaver*, the novel which in substance more resembles *The Viking Heart*, is technically unsatisfactory. Her canvas is much too large, the numerous families whose fortunes she follows are insufficiently distinguished from one another. The old romantic strain is replaced by a kind of unmotivated bitterness which finds release in a vehement out-crying against the stupidity of war. But in the end the romantic spirit reasserts itself; and the young hero Manfred, a modern Viking, learning that his fiancee has been killed in a bombing raid coincidental with one which he himself has led, flies away out to sea to meet his death in the sunset.

The Viking Heart is already almost as much a part of Canadian literature as *Maria Chapdelaine*; and indeed the two books have much in common. Both create the same illusion of reality; both are suffused with a kind of idyllic charm which tends to soften harsh outlines, and perhaps blur one's critical evaluations. And though *The Viking Heart* may not tell us the whole story of the Icelandic immigration or of the people who were a part of it, we must thank Mrs. Salverson for confirming in us one of the convictions of our youth — that the Viking heart is synonymous with all that is fine and noble and heroic in the human spirit.

IV

Of the few writers of Ukrainian ethnic origin who have attempted to interpret their people and dramatize their struggles in fictional form, Vera Lysenko is perhaps the most widely known. But whether the form is the one best suited to Miss Lysenko's talents seems doubtful on the evidence of her two novels, *Yellow Boots* (1954), and *Westerly Wild* (1956), particularly when they are contrasted with *Men in Sheepskin Coats*, her sociological study of the integration of various Ukrainian communities of western Canada into a regional culture to which they are making a significant contribution. *Yellow Boots* is devoted mainly to descriptions of various aspects of Ukrainian culture as they find expression in a prairie community; and the pallid love story which provides a thread of plot is much of the time buried out of sight beneath a welter of folkways embroidery.

Westerly Wild shows some advance in technique. Here the impact of the great depression and drought of the 1930's on a polyglot rural Saskatchewan community is at times effectively realized; but the novel as a whole is seriously marred by Miss Lysenko's seeming inability to tell a convincing story. The basic plot situation in *Westerly Wild* appears to owe more to *Jane Eyre* (including the mad wife in the attic) than to anything the author could have experienced or observed in life. But there is some good writing in individual scenes, and most notably in the conclusion when the hero-villain (Heathcliff crossed with Rochester) is crushed to death beneath the hooves of the great horses over whom he has for so long exercised ruthless mastery.

V

Religious communities have played a significant and at times dramatic part in the opening of the Canadian west. Men and women who by reason of the extreme or unconventional nature of their religious beliefs invited persecution in their homelands, found on the great plains room enough, so they believed, to live in deliberately sought isolation, insulated by distance from the contamination of worldly ways. The most spectacular of such immigrant groups is of course the radical Doukhobor sect known as the Sons of Freedom, whose addiction to nude parades as a form of protest against government authority has aroused world-wide interest and curiosity. Thus far, though, the Sons of Freedom (and the Doukhobors generally) have attracted the attention, among writers, of the historian and sociologist rather than the novelist. No significant work of fiction founded on life in a Doukhobor community, by either a Doukhobor or a sympathetic outsider, has as yet been written.

None the less, the struggle of a tightly-knit religious community to preserve its identity, its customs, and the practice of its intense and narrow religious beliefs when under pressure from indifferent or hostile outside forces represents the basic human plot-conflict in its most elemental form — the clash between spirit and flesh, God and devil. It is the kind of conflict that Tolstoi — who was intensely sympathetic to the Doukhobor cause and one of the sponsors of the Doukhobor settlement in Canada — might well have raised to the level of the universal had his religious speculations hardened into convictions while he was still at the height of his intellectual and artistic powers. As it is, *Resurrection,* written when Tolstoi was well past that height, is an impressive dramatization of faith enduring under persecution.

So far the most ambitious attempt by a Canadian novelist to dramatize the conflicts originating in the determination of a religious sect to maintain its integrity in spite of worldly snares and pressures is Rudy Wiebe's *Peace Shall Destroy Many* (1962). Wiebe, a native of Alberta, is himself a member of the Mennonite sect (in western Canada mainly of Ukrainian ethnic origin), one of whose basic tenets is pacifism. He is thus one of the very few who have written in any form of such a conflict from the inside.

Peace Shall Destroy Many specifically dramatizes the moral dilemma of a Saskatchewan Mennonite community during the Second World War. The older members are firmly rooted in the ancient faith and dedicated to the principle of non-violence. But the young have weaker roots. They are more conscious of the outside world than their elders and as a result of its attractions and pleasures they suffer from a sense of dislocation. They cannot accept with assurance the new world, but they are no longer at ease in the old.

The pitfalls which beset the author of a thesis novel are numerous, and Rudy Wiebe stumbles into several of them. In creating representatives of two conflicting attitudes and viewpoints he rather obviously loads the dice. Peter Block, the community deacon and spokesman for the traditional unwavering orthodoxy is a tyrant in his own family and a man capable of acts of appalling brutality. Inevitably the sympathy of the reader is directed to the side of gentle young Thom Wiens, symbol of disturbed and restless youth, regardless of the spiritual or philosophical validity of his position. Further, in his presentation of conflicting viewpoints Wiebe runs into serious technical difficulties which he is not always able to resolve. Thus lengthy debates alternate with scenes of unrestrained sadistic violence, as if the author were seeking to compensate with extravagant melodrama for the tedium of sustained argument and exposition.

Whether Wiebe can communicate character on anything approaching the universal level must remain in doubt. One suspects that in *Peace Shall Destroy Many* he has said all that he wishes to say about his own Mennonite people; and the non-Mennonite characters in the novel are cardboard cut-outs.

Wiebe's second novel, *First and Vital Candle* (the title a rather inappropriate borrowing from Gerard Manly Hopkins) emphasises Wiebe's unfortunate inclination to subordinate the living flesh to the moral or theological or sociological thesis. The central character, Abram Ross, an Arctic company man in charge of a store in a far-north Ojibway settlement, and his ruthless opponent, an independent trader named Sig

Bynnesen, at times evince a fluttering breath of life; but Ross's supporting cast, which includes a missionary couple and a hard-praying spinster schoolma'm, are no more than devices for the propagation of views interesting only to those readers to whom religion and morality are matters of narrow sectarian concern.

VI

Adele Wiseman's *The Sacrifice* (1956), a novel of international reputation, is less concerned with group issues than with that of the individual soul seeking to maintain an ancient and beloved tradition against the erosive forces at large in a new and alien world. Abraham, a Jewish butcher who is the victim of murderous persecution in his native Ukraine — his two eldest sons were hanged for no other reason than that they were Jews — comes with his wife Sarah and surviving son Isaac, to a prairie city readily identifiable as Winnipeg. "The important thing now," he says, "is that we must stop running away from death and from every other insult. We will seize our lives in these scarred hands again." In the new land they are free of the threat of death; their physical hardships are trivial by comparison with those they endured in their own country; and direct insults are rare, for the Gentiles who impinge on the Jewish community are generally tolerant, never actively hostile. The basic conflict which bedevils Abraham and his people is confined within the limits of the Jewish community — even more specifically within the limits of a single family; it is fought out between Abraham, who stands foursquare for traditional family solidarity and the authoritarian order of life (*his* authority supreme in the household even to the second and third generations), and his son, his son's wife and his grandson, who seek to relax the family bonds and live free lives.

The weakness of the average novel based on such a plot-conflict usually stems from too great a concentration on the central father-figure, so often a creature of such monstrous selfishness and perverse impulses as to cast all those over whom he looms into a shadow from which they never emerge to be clearly seen. No such weakness shows itself in *The Sacrifice*.

Abraham is in some ways blind and selfish but he is no monster, no Mr. Barrett of Wimpole Street in a butcher's apron. He is a warm-hearted human being capable of attracting love and of loving greatly; nor is his boast that he is receptive to new ideas — "I myself am a man who has always looked to the new, who is always willing to learn" — entirely without substance. But the area within which he is willing to learn new things is sharply defined; it does not encompass religious belief ("I remember a second cousin of my wife's who went mad and became a Christian"), nor family emancipation; and it is his inability to acknowledge the right of those closest to him to make their own decisions and plan the course of their lives that precipitates the ultimate tragedy. But no matter how much we may share his children's resentment of his seeming selfishness, his dictatorial ways, it is impossible not to be moved by Abraham's anguished cry when he feels himself banished by those whom he most loves — "The old can only crouch in a corner and pray."

All of Adele Wiseman's characters, even the least of them, are fashioned in the round from living flesh; each has a life of his own, dependent on individual personality and not on his relationship with a central dominating figure. Mrs. Plopler, the garrulous and unashamedly inquisitive Jewish landlady who takes the immigrant family into her home and is thereafter passionately involved in their triumphs and tragedy; Chaim Knopp the shoichet, a learned man who hates the chickens he kosher-kills ("I will go about like a ladies' man," he cries out in ecstasy when his wealthy son finances his retirement. "Years will pass — and I will never smell another chicken"); Polsky, Abraham's vaguely repulsive good-natured employer; Isaac, Abraham's tormented son, torn between scepticism and loyalty to a father whom he loves; Ruth, his strong-minded courageous daughter-in-law; Sarah, Abraham's wife, whose fading out of a life that has proved too much for her is recorded in the most moving line of the novel — "Her life had become like a long conversation in which she had somehow said all that she had to say, and to which she was now even forgetting to listen"—; these and a dozen more live by reason of Adele Wiseman's ability to communicate human nature in its infinite variety and multiple shades, and not by tricks of the caricaturist.

Only the sensuous *femme fatale* Laiah, whom old Abraham kills in a moment of frenzy when she attempts to seduce him, fails to carry complete conviction; she exists less as a human being in her own right than as the essential agent to precipitate the final catastrophe. The murder itself is the climactic plot-episode; it is in effect the sacrifice which leads by devious ways to Abraham's reconciliation with the surviving members of his family — his daughter-in-law Ruth and his grandson Moses — and for all three a measure of understanding and peace.

The Sacrifice is a model of competent craftsmanship. There are no fumblings here, no indecisive movements, no faltering of plot-line, no inconsistencies of character, no sacrifice of truth for sensation. With the single exception of the murder of Laiah every episode rises naturally, even inevitably, out of character; and it is possible to justify the murder — a deed which at first reading seems utterly at odds with Abraham's character — not as a deliberate act of the will but as an instinctive striking-out against a creature who has suddenly revealed herself to the hitherto unsuspecting old man as one who is in his eyes an obscene monster.

Most important of all, *The Sacrifice* is a novel which demonstrates that it is possible to present the problems of the tradition-ridden immigrant in a new land not as thesis but as drama.

Adele Wiseman's prose is unostentatious and uncluttered. It is a clean decisive prose which communicates with force and precision and at times great subtlety the impressions of one who looks at life clearly, not only through her own eyes but those of the people she creates. Few writers have suggested more vividly the impact of age-old landscape and new-born city on a sensitive mind and eye than does Miss Wiseman in recording the reaction she attributes to Isaac, Abraham's son, as he contemplates the city and the plain: "To Isaac the land seemed like a great arrested movement, petrified in time, like his memories, and the city crawled about its surface like a counterpoint of life."

Nellie L. McClung (1873-1951)

Until as late as the beginning of the First World War the
Canadian West retained much of the fascination of a pioneer
land; and the writers who caught something of its spirit, or
what the reading public in the East and the Old Country
romantically imagined to be its spirit, were usually assured of
a large following. No doubt there was a tendency among some
of these writers, understandable in the light of existing
temptations, to exaggerate the frontier virtues of courage,
hospitality, independence, and a strong sense of humour which
expressed itself most characteristically in crude practical
joking. But although exaggerated in the telling these virtues
were not mythical; the records of the old-timers, and the very
strength of the tradition which perpetuates them, afford sure
proof of their existence. They were associated, it is true, with
qualities not so desirable, including a strongly materialistic
outlook inevitable in a society made up entirely of men and
women involved in the struggle for daily bread, and — perhaps
because the struggle was so unrelenting — a certain callousness
and insensitivity towards the weaklings and the misfits.

So far, no writer has given us a really balanced picture of
the prairie pioneer, in which virtues and vices are emphasized
in their proper proportions. But Mrs. Nellie McClung, in her
modest short stories and novels, has done full justice to the
virtues. Particularly effective is the manner in which she
suggests the tremendous ebullience of spirit which character-

ized the Westerner in the boom period just before the First World War, when wealth seemed almost a certainty for every man willing to do an honest day's work.

Mrs. McClung's early successes, *Sowing Seeds in Danny* and *The Black Creek Stopping-House,* contain the best of her fiction. *Sowing Seeds in Danny,* ostensibly a novel, is actually a series of connected short stories recounting the trials and triumphs of a Manitoba small-town family, the Watsons, eleven stout souls who live in C.P.R. box-car No. 722 and such additions to the central structure as have been added from time to time to keep pace with the increase in progeny. The moving spirit of the Watson family is the eldest daughter Pearl, aged twelve, who embodies in her own small person all of the orthodox pioneer virtues, together with an innate appreciation of "the better things of life" which sets her apart from most of her acquaintances. Nearly all of the characters in *Sowing Seeds in Danny* are conventional romantic types — the Presbyterian Sky Pilot who marries the prettiest girl in town; the old doctor who has lost his grip and is drinking himself to death; the young doctor who performs a difficult operation on a kitchen table by lamp-light and pulls his patient through; the English remittance man with blue blood in his veins who is the butt of endless crude practical jokes; and half-a-dozen other types familiar to readers of romantic Western fiction. But there are one or two characters convincingly drawn, notably Sam Motherwell, the hard-bitten pioneer farmer whose god is money; and his shambling, ineffectual son Tom who, vaguely heart-sick for something better than the life he lives with his penny-pinching, insensitive parents, turns at last to a life of dissipation because, in the words of his creator, "when the powers of good are present in the heart and can find no outlet in action, they turn to evil."

Mrs. McClung's later novels do not entirely maintain the standard set by *Sowing Seeds in Danny* and *The Black Creek Stopping-House.* The story of Pearl Watson is continued in *Purple Springs,* but the young lady schoolma'am is a much less attractive and much less alive character than the engaging little gamin with the great heart and romantic outlook who is the heroine of *Sowing Seeds in Danny.* The grown-up Pearl is so imbued with crusading zeal on behalf of various causes that she develops into a rather tiresome and unconvincing reformer. This is not to suggest that the causes which she most enthusiastically espouses — Temperance and Women's Suffrage — are either futile or dull; only that Pearl's succession of triumphs over party politicians is a little too easy to be convincing. It is of course true that the triumphs ascribed to Pearl were in part at least Mrs. McClung's own; but while Mrs. McClung reproduces incidents from her own life vividly enough, she is unable to recreate in her heroine her own attractive and forthright personality.

Painted Fires, published in 1925 and dealing with the experiences of a Finnish girl in this country, is of some interest in that it is one of the few novels in Canadian literature which have as their theme the assimilation of the foreigner into the Canadian way of life. *Painted Fires* has enjoyed wide popularity outside this country, and particularly in Finland, where a translation was published in 1926.

Although Mrs. McClung's later fiction is hardly on the level of her earlier work, her best writing was done comparatively late in life. Her autobiography, *Clearing in the West*, published in 1935, is a wholly delightful little book, now well on its way to becoming one of the minor classics of Western Canadian literature. *Clearing in the West* is a serene, humorous and vivid account of that early West which Mrs. McClung in her various roles of school-teacher, house-wife and prominent public crusader knew so well. Her very real narrative power is nowhere more apparent; and she resists the inclination to point up her stories with an obvious moral lesson. But it is the people — idealized no doubt but tremendously alive — which constitute the greatest charm of the book. *Clearing in the West* is one of the few volumes of reminiscence about the Canadian West that deserve to endure.

Mrs. McClung was exceedingly modest about her literary work, and she would have been the first to agree that she never took her "art" seriously. Like Ralph Connor she did not look upon writing as an end in itself, but only as a means to an end. No doubt it is to her credit as a citizen genuinely anxious for the carrying-out of what she felt were

much-needed reforms that she was at all times prepared
to use the novel or the short story for the purposes of propa-
ganda. Indeed, it is fair to say that she conceived the novel to
be primarily an agent of reform. As such she has employed
it so effectively that her fiction is likely to be of interest to
the social historian for some time to come.

What Mrs. McClung has accomplished in her best work she
has herself summed up in words which she places in the
mouth of Mrs. Dawson, the heroine of an early short story,
You Never Can Tell. Mrs. Dawson, a prairie pioneer, goes
East upon the invitation of friends to address the Convention
of Arts and Crafts which is meeting in Ottawa. (It is, of course,
impossible to avoid identifying Mrs. Dawson with Mrs.
McClung herself.) Mrs. Dawson is not in appearance fashion-
able, and her hands bear evidence of much hard work. Her
old friends pity her because she lives isolated from the world
which really matters, from the centres of culture and comfortable living. But Mrs. Dawson quickly makes them forget their
pity:

Whatever the attitude of the audience was at first, they soon
followed her with eager interest as she told them, in her easy
way, simple stories of the people whom she knew so well, and so
lovingly understood. There was no art in the telling, only a
sweet naturalness and apparent honesty—the honesty of purpose
that comes to people in lonely places. Her stories were all of the
class that magazine editors call "homely, heart-interest stuff,"
not deep or clever or problematical — the commonplace doings
of commonplace people — but it found an entrance into the
hearts of men and women.

They found themselves looking with her at broad sunlit
spaces, where struggling hearts work out novel destinies, without
any thought of heroism. They saw the moonlight and its drifting
shadows on the wheat, and smelled again the ripening grain at
dawn. They heard the whirr of the prairie-chicken's wings
among the golden stubble on the hillside, and the glamour of
some old forgotten afternoon stole over them. Men and women
country born, who had forgotten the voices of their youth, heard
them calling across the years, and heard them, too, with open
hearts and sudden tears. There was one pathetic story she told
them, of the lonely prairie woman — the woman who wished she
was back, the woman to whom the broad outlook and far horizon were terrible, and full of fear. She told them how, at night,

this lonely woman drew down the blinds and pinned them close to keep out the great white outside that stared at her through every chink with wide pitiless eyes — the mocking voices that she heard behind her everywhere, day and night, whispering, mocking, plotting; and the awful shadows, black and terrible, that crouched behind her, just out of sight — never coming out in the open.

It was a weird and gloomy picture, that, but she did not leave it so. She told of the new neighbour who came to live near the lonely woman — the human companionship that drove the mocking voices away forever — the coming of the spring, when the world awoke from its white sleep and the thousand joyous living things that came into being at the touch of the good old sun.

The fact that Mrs. McClung does not show us what would have happened to the lonely woman—what in fact did happen to many lonely women — had the friendly neighbour not shown up, is illustrative of one of her more serious artistic weaknesses—her refusal at times to carry events to their logical conclusion. But this refusal is perhaps not so much sentimentality on Mrs. McClung's part as honest conviction. She was always a robust optimist, with a shining faith in the ultimate working out of all things for the best.

There is little to what Mrs. McClung says of Mrs. Dawson's speech that the critic can add by way of comment on her own fiction. Except, perhaps, that her outlook on life is as cheerfully realistic as that of twelve-year-old Pearl Watson, who in a fit of fine poetic frenzy wrote in her diary:

> *The little lams are beautiful,*
> *There cotes are soft and nice,*
> *The little calves have ringworm,*
> *And the 2-year olds have lice.*

II

Arthur Stringer (1874-1950)

A few years ago there appeared in a well-known Canadian periodical an entertaining little short story, *The Pot-Boiler,* which told of the abortive effort of a popular writer to escape from hack-work so that he might devote himself to the creation of "serious" literature:

"I'll tell you why I killed off the Rat, Summers," Stryker said into the telephone. "I killed him because I'm off the gangster stuff. Yes, sir, for life. Don't think I'm going highbrow on you. But this time I want to get out of the pulps. I want something closer to life. And I've got a serious novel with a serious problem to work out. Sure I know what the Rat's done for me. And for you, too. But he's dead and he's going to stay dead."

But Junior falls ill — pleural pneumonia the doctor says. Special nurses and oxygen tanks are needed "for the sulpha reaction has not been good." Stryker, after urging that no expense be spared, calls his agent:

"You know, Summers," he said over the wire, "I was wrong about the Rat. I believe I could bring him back and get a swell story out of a kidnapping sequel. Yes, kidnapping. Have 'em carry off a child, an only child, then play up the anguish of the parents and now they're on the anxious seat until the Rat's rounded up and the Kid's brought back. You're right; it's sure-fire stuff."

And the story ends with a picture of Stryker, three weeks later, glancing out of his study window at Junior who is out on the lawn with his mother, then turning to his typewriter to pound out the words:

The Rat, swinging down from the fire-escape with the child under one arm, crouched low as he reached for his automatic. But the watchful Westlake was too quick for him. With what looked like one and the same movement he brought his clubbed revolver down against the sallow skull of the gangster and wrested the child from the snarling Rat!

The author of *The Pot-Boiler* was Arthur Stringer. It is not too much to suggest that with a few modifications Stringer and Stryker are the same person. "You can't bring up a family on iambic pentameter," Stringer, a possibly frustrated poet, is reported to have said. Certainly he never shared the romantic notion that the artist should be ready to live in a garret if need be for the sake of his art. Stringer always wrote for public approval, and the measure of his success was such as to make him one of our best popular professional writers. He published over forty novels, a dozen volumes of poetry, innumerable short stories and articles, besides writing several movie scenarios. His largest audience has been in the United States, where he made his home for many years. But he was born and brought up in Canada; his themes have been prevailingly Canadian; and our claim upon him as a Canadian writer cannot be seriously questioned.

Stringer is a competent popular writer who usually writes about sophisticated people placed in unusual and difficult circumstances. When, inspired by some rather haphazard ranching experiences, he wrote a trilogy of Western novels, *The Prairie Wife* (1915); *The Prairie Mother* (1920); *The Prairie Child* (1922); which won for him the largest audience he has ever enjoyed, it was not surprising that his main characters were not native Westerners but sophisticates transplanted from a society which Stringer knew well and understood. The plot of the trilogy has to do with the struggles of Chaddie and Duncan Argyll McKail to establish a home on the prairies, rear a family and win for themselves happiness and security. Their failure to do so is not Chaddie's fault. She works hard, with unfaltering good humour and courage, does more than her share of hard work at Casa Grande — as the farm is grandiloquently called — falls in love with another man but buries her secret in her heart, and, until Duncan's behaviour transgresses the utmost limits of decency, is in all things a true and loyal wife.

But Chaddie's husband, Duncan Argyll McKail, is a humourless individual with a dull, bourgeois soul. His god is Mammon; and when his grandiose schemes go awry he sulks like a small boy. Moreover, he has a wandering eye. He is handsome, susceptible to flattery. But honest Chaddie does not flatter. Neither does she share his material ambitions. So it is that the marriage at last goes on the rocks. Chaddie's love for her husband, deep and genuine though it is, dies at last of sheer starvation; and the reader leaves Duncan in the cheerless grandeur of his city mansion and returns with Chaddie to the farm on the prairies and to the other man whose wife she will be as soon as the decree becomes absolute.

That Stringer's trilogy does not rise above the level of an ephemeral popular success is not in any way due to the author's lack of technical skill. Chaddie's story is told in the first person, through the medium of letters and diary; and it is told well. Indeed, Stringer's almost urbane competence in the mechanics of story-telling is in marked contrast to the rather clumsy technique which mars the work of so many of our novelists. But the story, even though told with the utmost skill and zest, fails to convince. The characters are all either exotics or caricatures. Not one is in harmony with his environment. The heroine Chaddie is a cultured New England society girl whose wit is reminiscent of a gay nineties salon. Her knowledge of painting, music, literature and human nature — and it is much to Stringer's credit that he makes this knowledge genuinely a part of her — is encyclopaedic. "Gershom's still in the era where he demands a story in the picture and could approach Monet and Degas only by way of Messonier and Bourgerau" is the kind of sentence that trips casually off Chaddie's tongue. After an evening of back-breaking toil, when the three children are tucked into their cots, she refreshes herself at the piano with a little Debussy, a little Chopin, and a great deal of Beethoven. And Duncan Argyll McKail, dull dour soul though he is, is quite at home in this kind of milieu. In his verbal exchanges with Chaddie — and they are numerous and prolonged — he is able to parry and riposte with a dexterity which leaves the reader painfully aware of his own conversational inadequacies. "I'm sorry you see only my bad side," says Chaddie. "But it's kindness that seems to bring out everything that is best out of us women. We're terribly like sliced pineapple in that respect: give us just a sprinkling of sugar, and out come all the juices." And Duncan replies quick as a wink: "That's a Chaddie McKail argument. And a Chaddie McKail argument impresses me as suspiciously like Swiss cheese; it doesn't seem genuine unless you find plenty of holes in it."

The Other Man, Peter Ketley, is also quite at home in the midst of this sort of thing. He carries a well-thumbed copy of

Marius the Epicurean in his overalls pocket; and the subtlest allusion to a Henry James character does not escape him. Even the first of the Other Women, Lady Alicia Newland, although devoted chiefly to the active traditional pursuits of her class — huntin', fishin', shootin' — is familiar with Theocritus and Marcus Aurelius. And she no doubt missed the Henry James allusion only because Chaddie discreetly lowered her voice in making it.

What it all amounts to is this; that the major characters of the trilogy — particularly Chaddie — have just a little of the charm and wit of Oscar Wilde's bright young men and women. And they are even less real.

Because the protagonists are basically unreal, it is not easy to feel the tragedy of Chaddie's broken marriage. In the first two volumes of the Trilogy, *The Prairie Wife* and *The Prairie Mother,* the gradual disintegration of the marriage relationship is traced with genuine psychological insight. The difficulties and disappointments of the early years help to create tensions not easily resolved; quarrels become more and more frequent and severe; and the stubborn streak in both is broadened and deepened rather than diminished as the years go by. Duncan's jealousy of his own children, who he thinks have won Chaddie away from him and so deprived him of a companion and mistress, is realistically suggested. But we are not prepared for Duncan's complete moral collapse, for his transformation from a rather stupid but essentially good-intentioned and slightly bewildered husband into a sadistic tyrant. Nor can the transformation be wholly justified on the grounds that Duncan's appearance in his unmotivated role provides what is perhaps the most dramatic scene in the entire trilogy. Duncan, bent on horse-whipping his little son for some trivial offence, finds his way barred by an outraged Chaddie, ancient Colt revolver in hand. When he refuses to heed her command to stop she pulls the trigger. The revolver is empty; but the effect on both Chaddie and Duncan of the appalling realization that she stood ready in her moment of madness to kill the man whom she had married is described with fine dramatic skill.

The final picture of a grossly fat Duncan McKail smoking

an expensive cigar and swilling alcohol before going down to the office where his paramour is waiting for him, leaving Chaddie to return by herself to the farm — where Peter is waiting for *her* — is so crudely melodramatic as to outrage the sensibilities of all but the most insensitive reader. But the picture is not without an element of poetic justice. After all, what end could be more appropriate for a tousle-headed six-footer who permits his wife to call him Dinky-Dunk?

What holds us to the trilogy — and assuredly none of its parts is ever dull — are the fine individual scenes — the prairie fire, the search for a small boy who is lost, the capture of a murderer — and the shrewd if occasionally superficial observations which Stringer makes, through Chaddie, on Western life and manners.

But in spite of occasional moments of perceptivity Stringer does not convey any strong impression of a peculiar regional atmosphere. The prairie is a convenient back-drop for the action of his stories but not an essential complement: the plot of the trilogy is one which could have been developed almost without modification in any setting the author had chosen to create. Of the profound influence of environment on human behaviour, an influence which to anyone thoroughly familiar with the Western scene is unmistakable and all-pervading, there is little evidence in Stringer's work. Perhaps this is the reason why the trilogy fails at the point which is the justification of the novel's existence. It does not communicate the sense of life.

III

Robert J. C. Stead (1880-1959)

The rapid rise of the Wild West School of American fiction which reached its zenith in the sensationally successful stories of Zane Grey, naturally offered serious temptations to the Canadian novelist. Some writers now forgotten succumbed to these temptations; but there were a gallant few, including Nellie McClung and Robert J. C. Stead, who refused to be led astray by public enthusiasm for a synthetic West of sheriffs, bad men, good men and ranchers' daughters, preferring to give an honest picture of the prairie life as it appeared to them in their time.

Robert J. C. Stead, although born in the East, is a Westerner by upbringing; and it was in the West that, as teacher, journalist and author, he earned his livelihood for many years. He first attracted public attention through his verse, written in successful imitation of Robert W. Service. His early novels, *The Bail Jumper* (1914), and *The Homesteaders* (1916), attracted less attention than his verse collections; but the public gave an enthusiastic welcome to *The Cow Puncher*, published in 1918. *The Cow Puncher* has been the most successful of Stead's novels, selling over 70,000 copies.

Today it is not easy to account for the great popular success of *The Cow Puncher* and its immediate successor, *Dennison Grant*. *The Cow Puncher* had the good fortune, of course, to appear at a time when its sentimental and romantic qualities appealed strongly to a war-weary public; and *Dennison Grant* — which in spite of its fine opening chapters is one of the weakest of Stead's novels — was no doubt borne upon the wave of popularity which had been created by *The Cow Puncher* for Stead's work. In both novels the hero is a typical romantic type. Dennison Grant is "spare and well-knit," his figure has "a suggestion of slightness which the scales would have belied," and his keen, clean-shaven face is as brown "as the August hills." In *Dennison Grant,* and to a lesser degree in *The Cow Puncher*, Stead tries to mix social doctrine with romantic adventure, but the two prove as incompatible as oil and water. It is simply not possible to take seriously the lengthy exposition of social faith which is placed in the mouth of Dennison Grant and poured out to a pretty girl whose life he has just saved, on a moonlit night on the ranges. This is not to say that a Westerner has no social doctrine — far from it — only that he recognizes as surely as the writer of Ecclesiastes that there is a time to speak and a time to love.

It is much to Stead's credit that he did not attempt to capitalize, as he might easily have done, on the popular success of these two novels. Instead of emphasizing the sensational and romantic, he turned to the serious portrayal of the ordinary men and women of ordinary Western communities in their ordinary occupations. From 1920 on his popular reputation declined, almost certainly as a result of his choice of subject matter, for his technical skill steadily improved. Since 1926, the year of the publication of *Grain,* his best novel, he wrote little. And his long silence is to be regretted for Stead at his best was capable of excellent work.

Indeed, it is not too much to say that *Grain* just misses being one of the most important novels in Canadian literature. Stead's hero, Gander Stake, is an almost wholly convincing characterization. Gander is born on a Western Canadian farm. His physical environment is described with unfaltering vividness and accuracy, and the details of description are artistically justifiable because they are never extraneous to the character of the hero. Gander is not an unusual child. His complete ordinariness is his predominant characteristic. He goes to school rather unwillingly and learns nothing that has much permanent effect on him. For, as the author makes clear, Gander's interest is not in books or even in people but in the good earth itself:

Gander was dull; learning came to him with difficulty; books were bothersome, and he was not disposed to be bothered. After his first shyness had broken down he enjoyed mingling with the other boys; he gloried in the games at recess and during the noon-hour; he never wholly disliked any teacher, but he hated study. For Gander was a farmer born and bred; he had an eye for a horse and a knack with machinery; the mysteries of the self-binder he had solved before he was nine, but the mysteries of the cube-root he had not solved before he left school — nor since. He knew more than any of his teachers about the profession by which he was to make his livelihood, and he regarded their book-learning as non-essential and irrelevant — neither of which words he would have understood.

Anyone familiar with a farming community has met Gander Stake. There are thousands like him all over the West and wherever men earn their living from the soil. He is the man bound to the land not through force of circumstances, but through an inarticulate, all-powerful love of the earth itself.

Gander's attendance at school becomes more and more spasmodic; and after his tenth birthday ceases entirely. He grows rapidly into a "tall, thin boy, hump-shouldered from sitting huddled on his machine, grimy with oil and blear-eyed with dust; knowing nothing about the cube-root but able to harness and handle four horses abreast, and filled with the joy of man's accomplishment." Unlike his brother Jackie he is not much interested in the money to be made from farming. Jackie quarrels with his father over the question of wages and between them there is enacted the kind of petty tragedy that is of common happening in every farming community. But Gander never dreams of rebellion; he and his father understand each other; the land is what matters; the open-air life, the growing crops, the hum of the threshing-machine — these things are in themselves more important than bushels per acre or the price of wheat. And it is altogether characteristic of individuals of his type that although Gander is content to work long hours in the field, the idea of lending a hand, even when he has time, to his tired, work-worn mother, does not occur to him. It is not a question of the labour involved, simply that there are some jobs like washing dishes, milking cows and bringing in water and wood that a "man" does not do.

Because he finds the earth itself a satisfying companion Gander does not often seek the fellowship of his kind:

On afternoons when he was not needed about the farm he went skating on the lake, his thin figure a pathetic suggestion of loneliness, thinner than ever in its contrast with the great expanse of ice and the hills sprinkled white with snow and hoar frost which shouldered up from the lake to the prairies beyond. Yet Gander was never lonely; never in all his days on the farm and the prairie did Gander know the pang of loneliness.

Nor is he conscious of any serious personal deficiencies. He is a good farmer and takes pride in the fact. For those who value book-learning he has only honest scorn. Minnie, his pretty and extremely intelligent sister, twits him one day about his ignorance:

"Do you know the difference between a noun and a pronoun?" she demanded of her brother one evening at the supper table.

"Don' know as I do," Gander admitted, without apologies.

"Huh. Teacher'd call you a dunce."

"Would she?" said Gander. "Well, I know the difference between a Deering and a Massey-Harris across a fifty-acre field, an' I bet she don't an' you can tell her that for me."

Which, from Gander's point of view, is the completely crushing rejoinder.

As he grows older Gander asserts his manhood by discarding braces and adopting a belt, as "being more in keeping with man's estate." But the change is not an entirely happy one since in order to keep his pants up Gander is compelled to walk with a peculiar hitch which eventually becomes a permanent feature of his posture. He develops into a shrewd and successful farmer whose range of ideas seldom extends beyond the limits of his father's farm. But the outbreak of the First World War compels him to grapple with problems of greater magnitude than those of weed control and profitable crop rotation.

Stead examines Gander's attitude towards war with genuine psychological insight. In 1914 Gander is eighteen years old, six feet tall, and as callow in mind as he is awkward in body. He is not particularly afraid of dying; indeed on one occasion he demonstrates a degree of courage far above the ordinary level — but he simply does not understand what the war is about; and the discipline and lack of privacy which military service entails horrify him. So, in spite of the covert pressure exerted by public opinion and even his own family, and a direct appeal made by Jo Burge, the girl whom he loves, Gander stays at home. At first he takes comfort in the assurance that growing wheat is a patriotic duty; but as time passes he finds it more and more difficult to face old friends:

Growing wheat became a patriotic duty into which Gander fitted like a cylinder nut into a socket wrench. He could grow wheat and none of that "form fours" nonsense about it. True, there were some who refused to see in the growing of wheat the highest expression of service; some even who were frank enough to suggest that the prospect of a high price had more to do with the sudden increase in acreage than any patriotic motive. But Gander avoided argument and kept on with his ploughing, his seeding, his harvesting and threshing. He, who had been reared on the plains, with himself for a companion, more than ever receded within himself. He avoided company, he avoided discussion, he avoided trips to Plainville. As a matter of custom he continued going to church at Willow Green, but even there sometimes found eyes that bored him through and sent him home in a tempest of self-excuse.

Gander's boyhood sweetheart, Jo Burge, marries Dick Claus, a returned soldier. Gander in his own way tries to forget. It is at this point in the story that a serious weakness in plot structure begins to intrude. The Stake family had figured in one of Stead's earlier novels, *The Smoking Flax;* and the author makes the mistake of attempting to knit together the plot of *The Smoking Flax* and the story of Gander. But the earlier tale of Minnie Stake and Cal Beach is retold so sketchily that the attempted interweaving fails almost completely. Only the reader familiar with *The Smoking Flax* is likely to be able to follow with any comprehension the plot ramifications in the concluding chapters of *Grain*.

There is, too, an unfortunately sentimental ending to the novel. Under the influence of a beautiful and sophisticated city girl's interest in him, Gander suddenly awakens to a realization of his inadequacies, and goes off to the city to work in a garage and attend night school, no doubt in order to make himself worthy of the girl. But such an action is not consistent with the character which Stead has so honestly and convincingly created. If the reader is sure of anything it is that Gander will never leave the farm which has first claim on his heart. We can forgive Stead one or two earlier inconsistencies — Gander is twice carried away by the force of violent and unmotivated physical passion — but his refusal to carry events to their logical conclusion involves a sacrifice of artistic principle out of keeping with the prevailing spirit of Stead's work.

But although his behaviour is thus not always convincing, Gander Stake is one of the few living people in Western Canadian fiction. Stead knew the Westerner better than did most of his contemporaries, and in *Grain* he develops a character who, up to a point of type, is none the less a complete individual. It is, too, a significant reflection of Stead's genuine skill in characterization that the minor figures in *Grain* —

Fraser Fyfe, Jackie Stake, Bill Powers the thresherman, Grit the hired man who has been around, and half a dozen others are all sharply distinguished from one another. Each is in some degree an individual with a distinctive personality. It is a pity that in the second half of the book Stead burdened himself with a conventional and distracting plot. The chronicle of Gander Stake and his neighbours is in itself of sufficient interest to hold the attention of most readers.

The defects in Stead's novels are often serious. His story-telling power is limited, his prose style not always apt to his subject matter. But among Western Canadian novels *Grain* is a noteworthy achievement. For with unusual courage Stead has chosen as hero of his novel a character distinguished only by reason of his complete ordinariness; he has traced, with sureness of touch and sympathetic insight, his development in relation to his environment; so that in the end Gander becomes that rarest of creatures in Canadian fiction—a human being in whose existence it is possible whole-heartedly to believe.

IV

Sinclair Ross (1908-   )

The Canadian novelists who, like Ralph Connor, wrote at a time when the West was thought of by outsiders as pioneer territory, were fortunate in that they were able to attract an audience for whom the prairies still held something of the fascination of the novel and far-away. The writers of the twenties, too, were fortunate in that they wrote at a time when the unusual intellectual ferment of the period, combined with very considerable purchasing power on the part of the public, created a demand for books without precedent in the history of Canadian publishing. But the novelist who had to battle for recognition in the hungry thirties worked in a different and less happy milieu. There was no falling-off of public interest in books; for many a man who had formerly given no thought to literature acquired a taste for reading during long hours when the public library was his refuge from a cold and jobless world. But since it is human to forgo the lifeblood of a master spirit for daily bread and butter, there was no money to spend on books. So it was that the Canadian writers who established themselves during the thirties were few in number and endowed with more than usual perseverance.

The West suffered more than most regions of Canada during the bitter years, for the miseries of drought were added to those of economic depression. But at least the thirties were years that gave men something to write about even though they were able to find few markets for what they wrote. And one Canadian, a young Winnipeg bank clerk, wrote some things about those years that are worth remembering.

How much Sinclair Ross had actually written is his own secret. But he had published very little — a few short stories, the best of them in the *Queen's Quarterly*, and two novels. His first novel, *As for Me and My House* (1941), sold only a few hundred copies and attracted almost no critical attention. Yet it is probably true to say that *As for Me and My House* and Ross's few short stories comprise the most significant body of prose fiction so far written about the prairie and its people. (Ross's second novel, *The Well* (1958), is a wildly melodramatic tale of the murder of an elderly prairie farmer by his young and monstrously evil wife who hopes to share her bed with the handsome young hired man, and must be dismissed as a comparative failure.)

It is understandable that *As for Me and My House* should have created no great stir. The theme is a modest one, the characters neither convincing nor lovable. The hero, Phillip Bentley, is a frustrated clergyman who has entered the Church only because it seemed to offer him means to the education which he coveted. Potentially a fine artist, he spends his life in one dreary prairie town after another carrying out priestly duties for which he has neither inclination nor ability. We see Phillip through the eyes of his wife, who tells the story of his struggle to escape from a detested environment. Ross uses the medium of the diary and letter for the telling of the story; and his handling of the medium is at times reminiscent of Stringer's technique in his prairie trilogy. Mrs. Bentley is in many ways like Chaddie McKail; she is a talented musician and a witty, courageous woman; but unlike Chaddie she is content to submerge her personality in that of her husband so completely as to become something less than human. When Phillip is unfaithful to her, her sole concern seems to be that he shall not suspect that she knows: when the illegitimate child of whom Phillip is the father is born, she insists that she and Phillip adopt it. This, surely, is carrying devotion to a point which even Patient Griselda herself would have found slightly ridiculous.

Phillip himself is a curiously wooden character. He is seen by the reader so many times in one characteristic action, that of stalking, white-lipped and silent, into his study and shutting the door against the world — which incidentally includes his wife — that after a while he becomes a kind of automaton going with mechanical precision through a limited series of movements. And all of the major characters are like Phillip in that they are almost wholly static; we know as much of them in the first paragraph as we do in the last.

Yet it would be blindness to deny the very great merit of *As for Me and My House*. For Ross shares with W. O. Mitchell the power to suggest the atmosphere of a prairie region which the reader, whether or not he is familiar with the Western scene, finds wholly convincing. A sentence or two illuminates the life of an entire community: "People in a little town like this grow tired of one another. They become worn so bare and colourless with too much knowing that a newcomer like Phillip is an event in their lives." And the descriptive passages are sometimes beyond praise. Even the most unimaginative of readers must feel the grit between his teeth when he reads such paragraphs as these:

There was a hot, dry wind that came in short, intermittent little puffs as if it were being blown out of a wheezy engine. All round the dust hung dark and heavy, the distance thickening it so that a mile or more away it made a blur of earth and sky; but overhead it was thin still like a film of fog or smoke, and the light came through it filtered, mild and tawny.

It was as if there were a lantern hung above you in a darkened and enormous room; or as if the day had turned out all its other lights, waiting for the actors to appear, and you by accident had found your way into the spotlight, like a little ant or beetle on the stage.

I turned once and looked back at Horizon, the huddled little cluster of houses and stores, the five grain elevators, aloof and imperturbable, like ancient obelisks, and behind the dust clouds, lapping at the sky.

The dust clouds behind the town kept darkening and thinning and swaying, a furtive tirelessness about the way they wavered and merged with one another that reminded me of northern lights in winter. It was like a quivering backdrop, before which was about to be enacted some grim, primeval tragedy. The little town cowered close to earth as if to hide itself. The elevators stood up passive, stoical.

The faults so apparent in *As for Me and My House* — the static characters, the artificial resolution of Phillip Bentley's dilemma (Judith, the mother of his child, dies in childbirth, and enough money is miraculously forthcoming from previous charges to enable him to buy a second-hand book-store in the city) — are not apparent in Ross's short stories. *The Lamp at Noon* is an almost unbearably real account of a prairie wife's mental collapse under the strain of the never-ceasing dust-storm, symbolized by the lighted lamp on the kitchen table at noonday; *A Field of Wheat* is one of the most graphic descriptions ever written of that cruellest of prairie phenomena, the hailstorm. In less grim vein but not less authentic are Ross's delightful studies of childhood and adolescence in *A Day with Pegasus* and *Cornet at Night*. But perhaps the best of his short stories — and certainly one of the best in Canadian literature — is *The Painted Door*, published in the summer issue of the *Queen's Quarterly* (1939).

Judged solely on the basis of plot, *The Painted Door* is sheer melodrama. The story is that of a wife's infidelity, and the tragic situation is resolved by the deliberate suicide of the husband in a blizzard when he learns the truth. But on another level *The Painted Door* is an admirable study of the effect of environment on character, and particularly on the relations between a man and his wife who have spent seven lean years on a Western farm where the wind blows incessantly and one bad crop season follows another with inexorable persistency. A single paragraph is sufficient to illustrate the skill with which Ross describes the kind of psychological tension which almost inevitably develops under such conditions and against which the individual is all but helpless:

> This now, the winter, was their slack season. She could sleep sometimes till eight, and John till seven. They could linger over their meals a little, read, play cards, go visiting the neighbours. It was the time to relax, to indulge and enjoy themselves; but instead, fretful and impatient, they kept on waiting for spring. They were compelled now, not by labour, but by the spirit of labour. A spirit that pervaded their lives and brought with idleness a sense of guilt. Sometimes they did sleep late, sometimes they did play cards, but always uneasily, always reproached by the thought of more important things that might be done. When John got up at five to attend to the fire he wanted to stay up and go out to the stable. When he sat down to a meal he hurried his food and pushed his chair away again, from habit, from sheer work-instinct, even though it was only to put more wood in the stove, or go down cellar to cut up beets and turnips for the cows.

A good measure of Ross's artistic achievement is to be found in his handling of a theme which might easily have degenerated into sordid sensationalism. His taste throughout is impeccable, his psychology sound. The wife's infidelity is not the consequence of a sudden yielding to momentarily felt passion; rather, it is the logical outcome of years of struggle and disappointment and defeat. Mistakenly she sees in the man Steven, and the Fate-ordained storm which has isolated them, a means of achieving some measure of compensation for all that the bitter years have denied her. With fine understanding Ross suggests the powerful psychological impulses which prompt the woman to give herself to Steven and which inevitably overwhelm her with remorse after the act has been committed.

The plot of *The Painted Door* is worked out with unusual care; and the denouement realized with stunning dramatic effect. Perhaps, when he reflects on the story in cold blood, the reader may feel that the ending is somewhat artificially contrived. But *only* after reflection in cold blood. For the actual time of reading at least, Ross wins from his reader that suspension of disbelief which constitutes not only poetic faith but proof of good story-telling.

Perhaps Ross's failure to achieve popular success is indirectly attributable to the man's integrity. Like his hero Phillip Bentley, instead of trying to make his work popular and saleable he has "pushed it somberly the way he felt it ought to go." Until recently there was reason to feel that Ross was a distinguished artist without honour in his own country, but within the last few years *As for Me and My House* has been recognized as a novel of superior merit and it is now preserved — one hesitates to say embalmed — in the Can. Lit. reading lists of our universities. And happily, the best of Ross's short stories have been rescued from obscurity and published in book form. They too should make the reading lists.

V

William O. Mitchell (1914-   )

The publication of William O. Mitchell's *Who Has Seen the Wind* (1947) is of unusual interest since it marked the appearance of a novel by a native-born Westerner which is above all else distinguished by a competent and original prose style. This is not to suggest that the book, which has enjoyed great popular success, is wholly to be praised. We may, for example, quarrel with the philosophic pretensions inherent in the prefactory note — "I have tried to present sympathetically the struggle of a boy to understand what still defeats mature and learned men — the ultimate meaning of the cycle of life"; we may protest that the small town in which the hero lives is peopled entirely by eccentrics and that no ordinary human being ever sets foot in it; we may feel that the deliberate contriving of comic incidents conceived in the broadest slapstick spirit and obviously intended to maintain "reader interest" is not the work of a responsible artist. But these weaknesses, serious though they undoubtedly are, should not blind us to the very real worth of Mitchell's achievement. In his story of small-town life as seen through the eyes and felt in the heart of a small boy, Brian Sean MacMurray O'Connal, he has expressed himself in a prose style which, for subtle cadence and freshness of imagery, is a delight to the mind and ear. "A dark wishbone of a child, wrapped in meditation" may, perhaps, be a little precious; but no one who has ever listened intently to the mutter of far-off thunder can deny the exquisite rightness of "the soft and distant explosions of light were accompanied by a sound as of lumber being dropped."

There are times, too, when Mitchell's descriptions of individuals reflect a glimmer of Dickens' genius for creating an instantaneous and powerful impression, although, like Dickens, Mitchell falls back on the art of the caricaturist in securing his effects:

> Mr. Palmer was a philosopher. A small man with black and almond-shaped eyes, his grey hair in tight ringlets close to his small round head, he made Digby think of a clown without grease-paint. His nose flared out at each side so that there were three distinct parts to it: it was as though a stalkless strawberry had been placed under the eyebrows liting up in perpetual surprise.

Mitchell's instinctive artistry is most apparent in his refusal to dramatize the drought. Brian O'Connal grows up in a small town in the centre of the dust-bowl where the crops are burnt up year after year. In the summer the street lights are often turned on in the middle of the afternoon. But the dust and the drought are not emphasized; and the effect of the drought on the community no more than hinted at. For Mitchell is writing of life as seen through the eyes of a small boy; and to a small boy growing up in the thirties in a southern Saskatchewan small town, heat and dust are a part of his familiar environment, to be accepted without question and without reflection. Brian's world is the town itself, and the town consists of people. The prairie beyond is Ultima Thule. What happens on its bleak waste does not concern him very much. Mitchell, whose understanding of the child's mind is extraordinarily sensitive, at all times avoids the mistake of interpreting the child's environment in terms of adult reaction.

William O. Mitchell is a writer of genuine and highly original talents. It is for this reason that *Who Has Seen the Wind* is likely to create in many readers a sense of dissatisfaction where a lesser work would leave them unmoved. For at times Mitchell seems prepared to exercise his talents in the deliberate creation of effects which lie outside the pale of responsible craftsmanship. Thus the triumph of the good schoolmaster Digby, over the forces of reaction and intolerance embodied in the person of Mrs. Abercrombie, the banker's wife, is a contrived "happy" ending to a long period of petty persecution, in which the reader may rejoice, but scarcely believe.

But the central theme suffers from no such aberrations; Brian Sean MacMurray O'Connal is to the end the creation of a writer whose sensitive understanding of a small boy's response to his environment is at all times matched by his fine taste in words.

Mitchell's subsequent work has, regrettably, so far failed to live up to the promise of his first novel. His *Jake and the Kid* stories, originally written for radio, commanded a wide listening audience, but they are essentially anecdotal, and the printed page denies them the support of the actor's voice and of the appropriate sound effects that are needed to give them life.

Emphasis on the anecdote at the expense of the overall design is in fact Mitchell's greatest weakness, and it shows at its most destructive in his second novel, *The Kite* (1962) published fifteen years after *Who Has Seen the Wind*. Its chief ingredients are the tall tale and the folksy character. David Lang, a journalist and TV panelist, comes to the foothills town of Shelby to write a story about Shelby's most celebrated citizen — Daddy Sherry, aged one hundred and eleven. Daddy's story is told partly through his own recollections, partly through relevant anecdotes which David Lang hears from various salty village types — the barber, doctor, minister and so on. All of the anecdotes are extended to greater length than their content warrants and several strain credibility to the breaking-point.

Mitchell presents Daddy on two levels — as a crusty cantankerous lovable eccentric and as a folk-hero who symbolizes the aspirations, virtues and history of an entire people. But legend and reality are always uneasy bedfellows; viewed in the hard clear light of a contemporary setting Daddy is not entirely convincing in either of the roles into which his creator casts him.

Perhaps because Mitchell's heart is at all times with Daddy and the village worthies his handling of the secondary characters, including the journalist, a small-boy philosopher and his widowed mother, is at best perfunctory. These people are stereotypes; only in rare flashes of illumination do they take on the life and colour one suspects Mitchell has the power to give them.

Although Mitchell fails to achieve the integration of his materials which is essential to the creation of a work of art there are occasional passages in the novel — the description of a goose hunt, of the making of a kite — as fine as anything he has written. Indeed *The Kite* is a novel of which it is true to say — Euclid to the contrary — that the parts are greater than the whole.

VI

Margaret Laurence

There are places of earth as familiar to us as our own plot of ground which are found on no map and reached by no road — Trollope's Barsetshire and Hardy's Wessex and Faulkner's Yoknapatawpha County and here in Canada the little town of Mariposa whose name is now honoured yearly by a festival of the folk. To such places of the earth, which combine a selection of existing physical features with those created to suit the author's particular intent, there may soon be added the prairie town of Manawaka. It is a town which lacks a precise geographical location, but any native westerner who reads Margaret Laurence's novels is able to identify Manawaka as the community he grew up in.

As a physical entity Manawaka is undistinguished, unobtrusive; indeed, it is the specific setting of only one of Margaret Laurence's novels, and nowhere is there a set description of its physical features. It exists primarily as an influence on the human spirit, it is a shaping force which either emancipates or stifles, give peace to or makes mad its creatures. Manawaka is a community neither rich nor poor; it is set near a river; it is well treed; life within its limits is moderately comfortable on the physical level; on the cultural and spiritual it is one or two removes above Sinclair Lewis's Main Street; but it suffers much from the kind of introversion which is an unhappy feature of small towns everywhere. Human contacts tend to be non-selective; people know one another too well, are absorbed by one another's affairs to the exclusion of larger interests. And because of this intimacy, this association with one's fellows within a closely-drawn circle, the person who grows up in Manawaka, unlike one who is the product of a larger more impersonal society, can never escape completely his environment.

Margaret Laurence is herself a native of Manawaka (specifically Neepawa, Manitoba). She has long since moved into the larger world lying beyond the horizons of the community she grew up in, she is a cosmopolitan, a citizen of the world, equally at home in its great cities and its desert places. (Perhaps her intense sympathy for Africa and its people derives in part from her prairie upbringing, for on the prairies, too, wind and dust and immense distances are familiar elements.) But wherever she goes, however she lives, she takes Manawaka with her; it is as completely a part of her, though less obtrusively so, as Egdon Heath is of Thomas Hardy.

The Stone Angel (1964) utilizes the Manawaka background through a familiar technical device—the operation of memory. Hagar Shipley, a woman in her ninetieth year, relives much of her earlier life in Manawaka through a series of flashbacks. The novel actually moves on two time planes, present and past juxtaposed. For Hagar the past is at least as significant as a present which in large measure she devotes to schemes intended to avert her incarceration in an old people's home. Hagar is gross of body, clumsy of movement, sometimes in the world of the present mentally confused. But the places and people of bygone years — Manawaka town; her sullen uncouth husband who loved land and horses better than he did people; her dead son John whom she helped to destroy; her father who owned the general store and was one of the town's most important citizens — these and a host of minor figures she recalls with that astonishing clarity which so often characterizes the mind of the very old when dwelling on things long past. And because they no longer impinge in any positive way on her life she recalls them with an occasional tendency to charitableness not apparent in her feelings and attitude towards persons immediately around her, most obviously towards her son and daughter-in-law with whom she lives.

From earliest childhood Hagar is a complex of impulses, hard-driven by a burning determination to be an individual in her own right. Her marriage to the handsome, semi-literate Bram Shipley is essentially an act of rebellion, a protest against a stultifying home environment which she can no longer tolerate. (" 'You think I'd allow you to go to South Manawaka and board with God knows who? You think I'd let you go to the kind of dances they have there, and let all the farm boys paw you?' " Thus her father, when Hagar asks permission to apply for a school a few miles from home.) In marrying Bram Shipley, a widower fourteen years older than she, Hagar moves from one extreme to the other, from one trap to another. Bram loves the land, he loves horses; perhaps, had she given him the chance, he might have loved his wife. But she gives him no such chance; she is contemptuous of him almost from the beginning of their married life; and even in extreme old age her recollections betray little softening of attitude beyond a half-hearted acknowledgement that things might have been better between them had she been a little kinder.

But Hagar by no means lives entirely in the past; and her concern with the present, almost to the end of her life, is consistent with her character. She has always been selfish, and in old age her selfishness manifests itself in an obsessive concern for her own comfort, and a contemptuous disregard of the needs of those who feel themselves compelled by the claims of family to look after her. But her selfishness is in a sense a defence mechanism operating against forces which she fears will isolate her from all familiar things; and her hostility towards her dull conscientious son Marvin and his equally dull conscientious wife Doris is intensified by vague guilt feelings which she cannot entirely suppress.

As her life nears its close — a close which she knows must be long drawn-out and painful — Hagar appears to undergo a change. In what is perhaps the most moving scene in the novel

she acknowledges the wrong she has done her living son
Marvin in favour of her dead son John.

"If I've been crabby with you, sometimes, these past years,"
he says in a low voice, "I didn't mean it."
I stare at him. Then, quite unexpectedly, he reaches for my
hand and holds it tightly.
Now it seems to me he is truly Jacob gripping with all his
strength and bargaining. *I will not let thee go, except thou bless
me.* And I see I am thus strangely cast, and perhaps have been so
from the beginning, and can only release myself by releasing
him.
It is in my mind to ask his pardon, but that's not what he
wants from me.
"You've not been cranky, Marvin. You've been good to me,
always. A better son than John."
The dead don't bear a grudge nor seek a blessing. The dead
don't rest uneasy. Only the living. Marvin, looking at me from
anxious elderly eyes, believes me. It doesn't occur to him that a
person in my place would ever lie.
Yet not a lie [she reflects later], for it was spoken at least
and at last with what may perhaps be a kind of love.

It is difficult, though, to believe that Hagar Shipley is now
ready to depart this life with calm of mind, all passion spent.
She has achieved a kind of peace, she has confessed (within
strict limits) the commission of sins; but the old Adam is still
strong within her, as when she says with grim humour, speaking of her conscientious daughter-in-law Doris, "Who will she
have to wreak salvation on when I'm gone? How she'll miss
me."
In his preface to his most successful novel, *The Old Wives'
Tale,* Arnold Bennett points out that "There is extreme
pathos in the mere fact that every stout aging woman was
once a young girl with the unique charm of youth in her form
and movements and in her mind. And the fact that the change
from the young girl to the stout aging woman is made up of a
number of infinitesimal changes, each unperceived by her,
only intensifies the pathos." The physical and mental contrast
between glowing golden youth and decrepit old age has
nowhere in Canadian literature been more effectively dramatized than in *The Stone Angel,* but the pathos of Hagar
Shipley's physical transformation is in a measure modified by

our realization that although she has lost her figure she has retained much of her original fire, her passion for life. There is really no need of the quotation from Dylan Thomas, which Margaret Laurence uses as an epigraph to *The Stone Angel,* to assure us that Hagar Shipley goes not gentle into that good-night.

"I've often wondered why one discovers so many things too late. The jokes of God." So Hagar reflects on certain episodes in her past, ironic twists of chance which so often defeat the purposes of men. One of God's jokes — what Hardy would call a satire of circumstance "because nobody intended it" — forms the basic plot-action of Margaret Laurence's second novel employing a prairie setting, *A Jest of God.* Here the locale is more precisely defined and restricted than in *The Stone Angel;* the action, covering only a few summer weeks, is set against the background of Manawaka town. In *The Stone Angel* Hagar roams in memory through many places within a time-span of nearly ninety years; but in *A Jest of God,* Margaret Laurence, consciously or otherwise observing the unities of time, place and action, imposes on her materials the design of ancient Greek tragedy. The result is a marked increase in the intensity of recorded experience with some loss of perception-range. Rachel Cameron's love affair, as fleeting as the short prairie summer, absorbs her to the point where she is blinded by its light and shadow to all that lies outside its narrow bounds.

Rachel Cameron is a schoolteacher in her early thirties who is trapped by circumstance (a semi-invalid mother) and temperament (an inherent timidity and an acquiescent disposition) into a life of dull routine from which escape seems a forlorn hope. Rachel is fully aware of her mother's petty tyranny, but lacks the will, the impetus to break away. At the age of thirty-four she is an edgy, restless, self-conscious woman whose sexual frustrations find an outlet in erotic dreams and self-stimulation (with accompanying guilt feelings), and on one occasion in a curious and by no means convincing hysterical outburst at a meeting of a religious sect whose members purport to speak in tongues. Rachel is not neurotic — a charge made against her by several presumably well-adjusted critics all of whom avoid defining one of the most misused terms in our language; her fears, frustrations and longings are in fact entirely normal for one of her age and circumstances. The decisive event leading to her emancipation is in itself commonplace, its consequences traumatic. She is seduced by a former schoolfellow who returns to Manawaka for a few weeks to visit his people. Rachel is not in love with Nick Kazlik in the full sense of the term; but he is male, self-assured, competent in the techniques of sexual intercourse, and the agent through whose offices Rachel is able to live for a few weeks the life of the "fulfilled" woman she so desperately longs for. For Rachel the sexual experience is so disturbing, so all-absorbing that it tends to obscure all else — even the man who provides it. It is logical that Nick Kazlik should remain to the end a shadowy creature, a sexual instrument rather than a well-rounded human being. (Incidentally, the sexual act is described primarily in terms of its significance for Rachel and the emotional consequences thereof, rather than as an exercise in gymnastics with accompanying technical and anatomical blue-prints.)

Within the span of those few short weeks Rachel experiences nearly the full range of the joys, the terror and the heartbreak of the woman insecurely, unhappily in love. Surprised by joy, made desolate by desertion, terrified by symptoms of pregnancy, paradoxically made further desolate by the removal of the cause of the symptoms (a benign tumour), she is indeed the victim of a sustained ironic jest. The love she welcomes with fearful eagerness proves at best no more than brief physical excitation and release, its consequences not security but insecurity, not peace but torment — and ultimately relief negated by a profound sense of deprivation and loss. The Biblical Rachel crying for her children is the universal symbol of mourning motherhood; but the Rachel of Manawaka town mourning her child unborn — indeed unconceived — is no figure of tragedy on the grand — hence purgative — scale, but the pathetic victim of an ironic twist of circumstance, one of the poorer jokes of God.

That Rachel, after her summer's experience, should find enough strength and resolution to break the bonds which hold her to Manawaka and her mother's way of life is entirely consistent with human nature. In loving Nick Kazlik, sharing with him the sexual act and enduring alone its probable consequences Rachel has tasted enough joy, suffered enough agony to make whatever ructions her leaving Manawaka might occasion seem but a little thing. But Margaret Laurence does not make the mistake of implying that in removing from Manawaka to Vancouver (where her married sister Stacey lives) Rachel will make for herself a new life, rich in the satisfactions of the flesh and the spirit which she has enjoyed fleetingly and still longs for. One lesson at least of universal application she has learned, which she articulates to herself when dreaming of possible marriage to a man she may some-day meet in the coastal city. "Maybe I will marry a middle-aged widower or a longshore man or a cattle-hoof trimmer or a barrister or a thief. And have my children in time. Most of the chances are against it. But not, I think, quite all. What will happen? What will happen. It may be that my children will always be temporary, never to be held. But so are every-one's." So much wisdom Rachel has learned from carrying a child in her womb which was no more than a benign tumour. One of God's poorer jokes, perhaps, but not without its illumination.

Life without marriage? The new Rachel faces the possibility without self-pity, but honestly, even with a certain wry humour:

I will remain the same. I will still go parchment-faced with embarrassment and clutch my pencil between fingers like pencils. I will quite frequently push the doors marked Pull and pull the ones marked Push. I will be lonely almost cer-tainly. I will get annoyed at my sister. Her children will call me Aunt Rachel and I will resent it and find then that I've grown attached to them after all. I will walk by myself on the shore of the sea and look at the free gulls flying. I will grow too orderly, plumping up the chesterfield cushions just so before I go to bed. I will rage in my insomnia like a prophetess. Some-times I will feel light-hearted, sometimes light-headed. I may sing aloud, even in the dark. I will ask myself if I am going mad, but if I do I won't know it.

Her last recorded thought is a reflection not only on her individual state of mind but on the human condition — and by implication on the nature of God himself: "God's mercy on reluctant jesters. God's grace on fools. God's pity on God."

Reluctant jesters. Those who learn to laugh, however wryly, in the face of the worst that life can do to them, accept it as an ironic joke. This much at least Rachel has learned to do in the course of a single summer.

It is significant that in *A Jest of God* the physical world of the prairies plays no overt part in shaping the character of Rachel Cameron. Hagar Shipley is in many ways the product of a pioneer community. Her fierce independence, her resourcefulness, her love of the wide earth and empty sky are obvious manifestations of a distinctive and unsophisticated environmental influence. Rachel Cameron, by contrast, is shaped by a small town environment which might be that of almost any small town on the continent—a community in which everyone is under everyone else's eye, in which one's goings and comings, deeds and misdeeds (particularly the latter) are under constant scrutiny — a self-contained self-absorbed unit of society in which the schoolteacher, next to the minister, is most vulnerable to attack. The struggle of man against his physical environment is no longer of much significance. Margaret Laurence's heroines, with the exception of the young Hagar Shipley, live in a society which has achieved a respectable level of material comfort; drought and depression and the loneliness born of isolation from one's fellows play no part in their lives. But universal aspirations, longings, passions do — together with that added twist of circumstance which may abet or frustrate the best-laid plans of men and women.

Margaret Laurence is content to use familiar situations for that revelation of human nature which is at all times her prime concern. The old man or woman re-living in memory a life now drawing to its close; the young woman seduced and abandoned — these are stock figures in literature. Indeed there are few more stereotyped situations in literature or life than that in which Rachel Cameron finds herself — seduced, apparently made pregnant, enduring the conventional tortures of the sensitive lonely woman trapped by love and facing imminent social disgrace. And Stacey, Rachel's sister (the heroine of *The Fire-Dwellers*, 1968) is involved in the familiar struggle to find some sort of justification of life while living the stultifying existence of a family-bound big-city suburbanite married to a man with whom she has little or nothing in common.

Not only does Margaret Laurence employ stock situations for the revelation of human nature, she is at times almost unbelievably clumsy in their resolution. Coincidence, absurd misunderstandings, mistaken identities are stereotyped devices, plot-clichés which she employs with a cavalier disregard of plausibility. These artistic blemishes no doubt reflect the author's impatience to get on with her real business — the revelation of her heroine's mind and heart. Thus Rachel Cameron misinterprets the significance of a snapshot of himself as a small boy that Nick Kazlik shows her. "Mine," he says, and Rachel believes that the snapshot is one of Nick's son. But what matters to the author and ultimately to the reader is not the misinterpretation, in itself scarcely credible, but the consequences for Rachel of the stunning revelation — as she believes it to be — that her lover is a married man and a father. Similarly, the termination of Rachel's pregnancy, through the removal of a benign tumour, may appear a preposterous resolution to what threatens to be a most difficult — possibly tragic — situation. But it must not be overlooked that before her operation Rachel has already experienced the agony of mind attendant upon a genuine pregnancy — as she believes her own to be — and has mustered courage to take the appropriate steps on the assumption that in a few months she will be the mother of an illegitimate child. Not the situation itself but Rachel's reaction to it is what matters.

Margaret Laurence's greatest gift — next to a compassionate heart — is a way with words. Her plots may be cliché-ridden but never her prose. Here, for example, is the local minister, as seen through Hagar Shipley's ninety-year-old eyes; "Doris is very religious. She says it is a comfort. Her minister is plump and pink and if he met John the Baptist in tatters in the desert, stuffing dead locusts into that parched mouth for food and blazing the New Kingdom out of those terrible eye-sockets he would faint." Marvin, Hagar's son, is disposed of in a sentence or two: "Doris pours more tea. We are comfortable. Marvin is hairy in shirtsleeves, elbows on the table. High dry or holiday or Judgement Day — no difference to Marvin. He would have put his elbows on the table if he'd been an apostle at the Last Supper." Clad in a hospital gown Hagar tells us she resembles "a perambulating pup-tent," and in a dozen words she creates an unforgettable vignette of the occupants of an Old People's home — "small ancient women, white-topped and frail as dandelions gone to seed."

An obvious element in these passages and in much of Margaret Laurence's work is a humorous irony which often extends through an entire scene. There is such a scene in *A Jest of God* in which Rachel, unable to sleep, goes late at night to the undertaker's parlour (once her father's) below the flat where she and her mother live, and drinks the undertaker's whiskey and listens to a lecture on the art of undertaking which is reminiscent — but in no way imitative — of Evelyn Waugh's *The Loved One.* Even more devastating, because more universal in its application, is Hagar Shipley's report of the conversation that ensues when Marv and Doris take her for an evening drive in the country:

All would be lovely, all would be calm, except for Doris's voice squeaking like a breathless mouse. She has to explain the sights. Perhaps she believes me blind.

"My, doesn't everything look green?" she says, as though it were a marvel that the fields were not scarlet and the alders aquamarine. Marvin says nothing. Nor do I. Who could make a sensible reply?

"The crops look good, don't they?" she goes on. She has lived all her life in the city, and would not know oats from sow-thistle. "Oh, look at the blackberries all along the ditch. There'll be tons of them this year. We should come out when they're ripe, Marv, and get some for jam."

"The seeds will get under your plate." I can't resist saying it. She has false teeth, whereas I, through some miracle, still possess my own. "They're better for wine, blackberries."

"For those that use it," Doris sniffs.

She always speaks of 'using' wine or tobacco, giving them a faintly obscene sound, as though they were paper handkerchiefs or toilet paper.

But soon she's back to her cheery commentary. "Oh look — those black calves. Aren't they sweet?"

If she'd ever had to take their wet half-born heads and help draw them out of the mother, she might call them by many words, but *sweet* would certainly not be one of them. . . . What I don't care for is her liking them when she doesn't understand the first thing about it. . . .

"Dry up, Doris, can't you?" Marvin says, and she gapes at him like a flounder.

"Now, Marvin, there's no call to be rude." Strangely, I find myself taking her part, not that she'll thank me for it.

Perhaps the scene derives a good deal of its impact from our uncomfortable awareness that Doris's conversational banalities, which serve no purpose other than to break silence, are part of a common stock from which we ourselves draw more often than we realize.

Margaret Laurence is a prolific writer and thus stands apart from most of her western fellow-novelists who after a novel or two are so exhausted from battling the elements — heat and wind and dust and drought — that they dry up completely and are never heard from again. She has been accused, perhaps fairly enough, of being too much preoccupied, through her heroines, with the miseries of being a woman (big hips not the least of these); and her use of a technique resembling dramatic monologue crossed with stream-of-consciousness, while highly effective in *The Stone Angel,* borders on the tedious in *The Fire-Dwellers.* There is little likelihood, though, that Margaret Laurence will be content to follow familiar ways, even though those ways may be of her own fashioning. In her short stories she shows sure command of a wide range of techniques and stylistic variations; and she is a cosmopolitan with an absorbing curiosity about the people among whom she lives and for most of them an unusual degree of empathy and understanding. She is thus admirably equipped at all points to communicate her vision of life.

But her roots are in Manawaka. One suspects that no matter how far she may wander into other places of earth Margaret Laurence will, like Hagar Shipley, return again and again in spirit if not in flesh to the commonplaces of her home town, finding in them — as she has already done more than once — substance for the creation of a universally significant work of art.

CHAPTER SEVEN

FUTURE INDEFINITE

The Canadian west is young. Its settlement began in a tentative way less than one hundred years ago, and its resources have been developed mainly in our own century. It is still sparsely populated, and only in recent years has industrialization, with accompanying urban growth, affected the nature of that development. Moreover, until after the Second World War the prairie population was distinguished by — among other features — extraordinary mobility. Few people settled on the prairies, and especially on the farm, with the firm intention of staying there for the rest of their lives. Their Mecca, or more accurately their Avilion — "where falls not any hail . . . or snow, or ever wind blows loudly—" was the Coast. Thither many of them retired after having made their money out of prairie soil.

A mobile population creates few traditions. Not that tradition is essential to the creation of great art, but it is an exciting stimulus to the imagination. Certainly its lack may have a notably depressing effect on a sensitive individual coming from a land where tradition is deep-rooted. Rupert Brooke, although impressed by the magnificence of the scenery on this continent, was not moved; had he lived among us he would probably have found little to write about. The feeling of newness troubled him. America — more specifically western America — was not for him the artist's domain:

Americans, so active in this life, rest quiet afterwards. And though every stone in Wall Street have its separate Lar, their kind have not gone out beyond city lots. The maple and the beech conceal no Dryads, and Pan has never been heard among these reed beds. Look as long as you like upon a cataract of the New World, you shall not see a white arm in the foam. A godless place. And the dead do not return. . . . The land is virginal, the wind cleaner than elsewhere, and every lake new-born and every day the first day. . . . There walk, as yet, no ghosts of lovers in Canadian lanes. This is the essence of the grey freshness and brisk melancholy of this land. And for all the charm of those qualities, it is also the secret of the European's discontent. For it is possible, at a pinch, to do without gods. But one misses the dead.

Thomas Hardy, too, would have been uncomfortable among us. Commenting on the dislocation of a rural community in the south of England, he described the consequences of the upheaval for the local artist in these terms:

The recent supplanting of the class of stationary cottagers, who carried on the local traditions and humours, by a population of more or less migratory labourers . . . has led to a break of continuity in local history, *more fatal than any other to the preservation of legend, folklore, close inter-social relations, and eccentric individualities*. For these the indispensible conditions of existence are attachment to the soil of one particular spot by generation after generation.

If Hardy is to be believed, population mobility militates against the development of that substantial body of legend, folklore, song and story which provides the foundation of a regional or national literature. Until a decade or two ago there was, however, little evidence to suggest that the rural population of the prairies was likely to become deeply rooted in the soil from which it made its livelihood. It is an enlightening and depressing experience to visit a well-remembered prairie community, familiar perhaps in childhood, after long absence. One will see few familiar faces, hear few remembered names. The graveyard tells the same story. The family plots are few and rarely hold the dust of more than one generation.

Prairie writers have shared the common urge to move from the sun-bleached brown plains to pastures where the grass grows green and tall. Hardly a single western novelist has remained true in flesh as well as spirit to his native heath. In an earlier time he moved away to seek fame and fortune in Toronto; now he gets himself a Canada Council grant and exchanges the snow-blanketed sod of Buffalo Gulch, Saskatchewan, for the hot sands of the Costa del Sol.

None the less, in spite of conditions seemingly hostile to the development of a soundly-based literature, the novel which draws its inspiration from the prairie locale has achieved a degree of sophistication and a stature not commonly associated with the creative arts in a thinly populated wind-blown region little more than half a century removed from the pioneer stage of development. Frederick Phillip Grove, Robert Stead, Sinclair Ross, Adele Wiseman, Martha Ostenso, Gabrielle Roy and Margaret Laurence constitute a group of novelists whose work compares favourably with that of regions of much longer settlement, larger population and greater wealth. It is surely significant that of the forty novelists represented in a paperback library of Canadian 'classics' — much the largest of its kind so far published in this country — no fewer than eighteen are either prairie born or have derived their inspiration from the prairies. In the light of this really remarkable progress it would seem reasonable to expect that with the novel tradition well established in western Canada, prairie novelists would continue to make a contribution to our literature of steadily maturing quality and deepening significance.

In the forties and fifties of our century, such an expectation might well have been justified on the grounds that westerners were at last taking roots. The urge to clean up fast and get out fast was being replaced by a more responsible attitude towards the land; a succession of excellent crops (partly the result of good weather, partly of scientific farming methods) and seemingly secure world markets gave the farmer money to spend on up-to-date conveniences for the family home; good roads and modern communications systems, including radio and TV, exorcised the old sense of isolation that had haunted first-comers, and there appeared to be at last emerging from the uncertainties and restlessness of earlier times a stable way of life, founded on the land, in most respects conformable to conventional contemporary trends but not entirely devoid of customs and developing traditions shaped by a unique physical environment — in short, a way of life which by reason of its stability and individuality was ideally suited to the fostering of the creative arts.

These fair expectations of a settled rural community have not, however, been fulfilled; instead, the family farm, from time immemorial the foundation of an agrarian society, has all but ceased to exist. The reasons for its rapid decline are fundamentally economic; in recent years the price the farmer receives for his produce has not kept pace with production costs. Only the large farm of many hundreds of acres, more and more frequently owned and operated by an impersonal syndicate whose headquarters may be in another country, seems able to pay its way. Today — most noticeably in Saskatchewan, once the breadbasket of the world — the scores of abandoned farmsteads visible from any well-travelled highway in the course of an hour's drive are bleak evidence of the passing of the old way of life.

Even on those farms where the family unit still survives the inevitable trend is to look to the nearest large town or city as the focal point of entertainment and cultural activity. The country schoolhouse, once the centre of community life in so many of its aspects — educational, cultural, religious, frivolous — has long since disappeared; farm children ride to town schools in buses, their parents shop in the town supermarket. Indeed many families who make their living farming have established permanent homes in town, leaving the original farm buildings to rot away behind neglected windbreaks.

The smaller towns are dying too. Built originally on the railroad eight or ten miles apart for the convenience of farmers driving horse-drawn outfits, many no longer justify their existence. The new highways pass them by; only the grain elevators standing tall against the sky and bulging with unsold grain enable them to maintain a tenuous life. But Main Street is more often than not lined on either side by empty rotting buildings and weed-grown lots, interspersed here and there with a few hardy perennials — gas station, grocery store, post office, Chinese restaurant. If there is a hotel it owes its continuing existence to its beer-parlour.

Men and women of an earlier day, who cannot afford to retire to the Coast, or bear to sever connections with their familiar environment, linger on in these dying villages; others of the older generation fill the admirably equipped Senior Citizens' or Pioneer Homes which are now found in most large towns. Few of these retired people — and this must surely be one of the most disturbing aspects of their old age — have any tangible connections now with their own past. Their children in most instances have long since gone far away and the family farm has been sold — merged with a larger unit as likely as not owned by strangers.

Out of these changed social and economic conditions has evolved a theme of possibly tragic implications which so far none of our novelists has attempted to dramatize — the divorcing of an entire generation from its own past.

By contrast with the prairie rural scene the urban community flourishes. Large towns are growing larger and the cities surge with hurrying life. More and more, industry is taking over from agriculture as the foundation of the western economy; oil wells dot many thousands of acres and Saskatchewan soil covers the world's largest deposits of potash.

II

What are the likely consequences for the arts — and especially the novelist's art — of this dislocation of a rural population and the startling acceleration of urban growth? Certainly any hope of Hardy's "substantial body of legend, folklore and story" being evolved in a stable community through a long process of accretion has been completely dissipated. The truth is, though, that the development of a substantial folklore is dependent not only on "an attachment to the soil of one particular spot by generation after generation" but limited education and unsophisticated outlook. From the beginning of western settlement the Church, the Law and the Little White Schoolhouse made the development of a substantial regional folklore an impossibility. Such tales and ballads with a western flavour as have circulated among us are rarely indigenous; nearly all have been borrowed from the folklore of the older American frontier.

Nor can it plausibly be argued that urbanization is necessarily a bad thing for the arts; in fact, the opposite is obviously true. Hardy spoke as a countryman in spirit who found the substance of his art in the soil and mores of his native heath, but Shakespeare left the small town for the great city, and the Lake Poets failed to find in nature a permanent source of inspiration. It has been said, and truly, that there are no literary cliques in the west as there are in the east, but this is not necessarily a good sign. Cliques have always flourished in urban societies where there is a lively interest in the arts. In the west the attitude of the general public towards the artist is one of tolerance but not always of understanding. The economic fight has been a peculiarly bitter one and the man who can play his part in that fight is the man who matters. What the artist does tends to be of value in proportion to its sales. And the artist, oppressed by an isolation which is often physical as well as spiritual, sometimes come to feel that the game is not worth the candle. There are probably few unfinished masterpieces mouldering away in bureau drawers because their creators got no encouragement from friends and fellow-artists, but it is reasonable to suppose that they may be found in larger quantity in the west than elsewhere in Canada. In the large urban centre the artist can always find a few of his own kind with whom he can collaborate in the publication of a modest periodical, thereby in some measure satisfying his need to communicate; but in most western communities outside the universities he must work alone.

It is significant that nearly all western novelists have either been the products of, or intimately associated with, the largest of our western cities — Winnipeg. The Manitoba capital has indeed a legitimate claim to being considered not merely the geographical but also the cultural centre of Canada. It supports a radically experimental theatre, the best symphony orchestra west of Toronto, a ballet company that enjoys a genuinely international reputation; and it is the birthplace, or at one time or another the housing-place, of more novelists, good, bad and indifferent, than can be matched by any other Canadian city. Not even Montreal or Toronto is able to challenge a list that includes Ralph Connor, Frederick Phillip

Grove, Martha Ostenso, Robert Stead, Laura Goodman Salverson, Adele Wiseman, Vera Lysenko, Jack Ludwig, Patricia Blondell (a splendidly original undisciplined talent who died much too soon), Gabrielle Roy (born and reared in St. Boniface) and Margaret Laurence.

It must, however, be a matter of some concern that no other western city is able to show anything like the same interest in the arts or approach the same level of achievement, perhaps because the only two which approximate to Winnipeg in size, Edmonton and Calgary, are at present frenetic boom-towns preoccupied with getting and spending, whose prosperity is founded on oil. Winnipeg has had its boom periods too, but its growth has been on the whole consistent, its fortunes most intimately associated with the land and its produce. In Winnipeg there has been more leisure for reflection than in most prairie cities. And of all prairie cities it derives its culture from the greatest number of ethnic sources.

III

So far the work of western novelists has been uneven in quality and in the main conventional in technique. But even the worst of it possesses a characteristic flavour born of the artist's involvement with a physical environment which makes a stunning impact on the transient visitor and haunts the native, however far away he may wander, until he dies. Industrialization and urban development may continue to pollute prairie streams and obliterate farmlands, but it is impossible to conceive of a time when the enormous vault of sky will be blotted out by smog and the great plains wholly defiled by man and his works. And if the prairie environment preserves a measure of inviolability there is reason to believe that it may someday foster a literature which will be a dramatization of the universal human condition. For if Thomas Hardy is right, in this age of bewilderment and frustration and hope that hardly dares to be, few places on the continent are more completely in harmony with the spirit of contemporary man. In that great first chapter of *The Return of the Native* Hardy says of Egdon Heath:

It was a spot which returned upon the memory of those who loved it with an aspect of peculiar and kindly congruity. Smiling champaigns of flowers and fruit hardly do this, for they are permanently harmonious only with an existence of better reputation as to its issue than the present. Twilight combined with the scenery of Egdon Heath to evolve a thing majestic without severity, impressive without showiness, emphatic in its admonitions, grand in its simplicity. The qualifications which frequently invest the facade of a prison with far more dignity than is found in the facade of a palace double its size lent to this heath a sublimity in which spots renowned for beauty of the accepted kind are utterly wanting. Fair prospects wed happily with fair times; but alas, if times be not fair! Men have oftener suffered from the mockery of a place too smiling for their reason than from the oppression of surroundings oversadly tinged. Haggard Egdon appealed to a subtler and scarcer instinct, to a more recently learnt emotion, than that which responds to the sort of beauty called charming and fair.

Indeed, it is a question if the exclusive reign of this orthodox beauty is not approaching its last quarter. The new Vale of Tempe may be a gaunt waste in Thule; human souls may find themselves in closer and closer harmony with external things wearing a somberness distasteful to our race when it was young. The time seems near, if it has not actually arrived, when the chastened sublimity of a moor, a sea or a mountain will be all of nature that is absolutely in keeping with the moods of the more thinking among mankind.

What Hardy here says of Egdon is, almost without modification, applicable to the prairie scene. It, surely, is a part of nature "absolutely in keeping with the moods of the more thinking among mankind." So far, the energies of its people have been devoted to the production of wheat and political parties. But it is not too much to hope that they will some day produce a book which the world will not willingly let die.